First World War
and Army of Occupation
War Diary
France, Belgium and Germany

32 DIVISION
Divisional Troops
Divisional Ammunition Column
28 December 1915 - 28 October 1919

WO95/2381/2

The Naval & Military Press Ltd
www.nmarchive.com
Published in association with The National Archives

Published by

The Naval & Military Press Ltd

Unit 10 Ridgewood Industrial Park,

Uckfield, East Sussex,

TN22 5QE England

Tel: +44 (0) 1825 749494

www.naval-military-press.com

www.nmarchive.com

This diary has been reprinted in facsimile from the original. Any imperfections are inevitably reproduced and the quality may fall short of modern type and cartographic standards.

© **Crown Copyright**
Images reproduced by permission of The National Archives, London, England, 2015.

Contents

Document type	Place/Title	Date From	Date To
Heading	WO95/2381/2		
Heading	32nd Division Divl Artillery 32nd Divl Ammn Colmn. Jan 1916-1919 Oct		
Heading	32nd Divisional Artillery. Disembarked Havre 30.12.15. 32nd Divisional Ammunition Column R.F.A. January 1916 To Dec 1918		
War Diary		28/12/1915	24/01/1916
Heading	32nd Divisional Artillery. 32nd Divisional Ammunition Column R.F.A. February 1916		
War Diary	In the Field	06/02/1916	25/02/1916
Heading	32nd Divisional Artillery. 32nd Divisional Ammunition Column R.F.A. March 1916		
War Diary	In the Field	02/03/1916	31/03/1916
Heading	32nd Divisional Artillery. 32nd Divisional Ammunition Column R.F.A. April 1916		
War Diary	In the Field	08/04/1916	28/04/1916
Heading	32nd Divisional Artillery. 32nd Divisional Ammunition Column R.F.A. May 1916		
War Diary	In the Field	20/05/1916	26/05/1916
Heading	32nd Divisional Artillery. 32nd Divisional Ammunition Column R.F.A. June 1916		
War Diary	In the Field	03/06/1916	30/06/1916
War Diary	In the Field	07/06/1916	19/06/1916
Heading	War Diary Divisional Ammunition Column, R.F.A. 32nd Division. July 1916		
War Diary	In the Field	01/07/1916	29/07/1916
War Diary	In the Field	01/07/1916	17/07/1916
Heading	32nd Divisional Artillery. 32nd Divisional Ammunition Column. R.F.A. August 1916		
War Diary	In the Field	05/08/1916	28/08/1916
Heading	32nd Divisional Artillery. 32nd Divisional Ammunition Column R.F.A. September 1916		
War Diary	In the Field	06/09/1916	28/09/1916
Heading	32nd Divisional Artillery. 32nd Divisional Ammunition Column R.F.A. October 1916		
War Diary	In The Field	01/10/1916	29/10/1916
Heading	32nd Divisional Artillery. 32nd Divisional Ammunition Column R.F.A. November 1916		
War Diary	In the field	02/11/1916	28/11/1916
War Diary	In the field	18/11/1916	30/11/1916
War Diary		06/12/1916	06/12/1916
War Diary		05/12/1916	29/12/1916
Heading	Confidential War Diary Of Divisional Ammunition Column R.F.A. From 1st To 31st January 1917		
War Diary	In the Field	04/01/1917	31/01/1917
War Diary	In the Field	29/01/1917	29/01/1917
Heading	War Diary Of 32nd Divisional Ammunition Column, R.F.A. From 1st February 1917 To 28th February 1917. Volume 14		
War Diary	In the Field	01/02/1917	25/02/1917

Heading	32nd Divisional Ammunition Column R.F.A. War Diary. From March 1st 1917 To March 31st 1917		
War Diary	In the Field	03/03/1917	31/03/1917
War Diary	In the Field	30/03/1917	30/03/1917
War Diary	In the Field	31/03/1917	31/03/1917
Heading	War Diary Of 32nd Divisional Ammunition Column, R.F.A. From 1st April 1917. To 30th April 1917		
War Diary	In the Field	01/04/1917	30/04/1917
Heading	War Diary Of 32nd Divisional Ammunition Column, R.F.A. From 1st May 1917 To 31st May 1917. Volume 17		
War Diary	In the Field	14/05/1917	18/05/1917
War Diary	In the Field	17/05/1917	31/05/1917
War Diary	In the Field	29/05/1917	29/05/1917
Heading	32nd Divisional Ammunition Column, R.F.A. War Diary 1-30 June 1917		
War Diary	In the Field	04/06/1917	26/06/1917
Heading	War Diary Of 32nd Divisional Ammunition Column, R.F.A. From 1st July 1917 To 31st July 1917. Volume 19		
War Diary	In the Field	10/07/1917	31/07/1917
War Diary	In the Field	30/07/1917	30/07/1917
Heading	War Diary Of 32nd Divisional Ammunition Column, R.F.A. For Period 1st To 31st August 1917		
War Diary	In the Field	03/08/1917	15/08/1917
Miscellaneous	Headquarters, 32nd Divisional Artillery.	05/09/1917	05/09/1917
Heading	War Diary Of 32nd Divisional Ammunition Column, RFA. Period 1st To 30th September 1917 Volume 21		
War Diary	In the Field	02/09/1917	27/09/1917
Heading	War Diary Of 32nd Divisional Ammunition Column, R.F.A. From 1st October 1917. To 31st October 1917 Volume 22		
War Diary	In the Field	08/10/1917	30/10/1917
Heading	War Diary Of 32nd Divisional Ammunition Column R.F.A. From 1st To 30th November 1917		
War Diary	In the Field	04/11/1917	30/11/1917
Heading	Confidential War Diary Of 32nd Divisional Ammunition Column, R.F.A. From 1st To 31st December 1917. Volume 24		
War Diary	In the Field.	02/12/1917	20/12/1917
Heading	Confidential War Diary Of 32nd Divisional Ammunition Column, R.F.A. 1st To 31st January 1918		
War Diary	In the Field	06/01/1918	31/01/1918
Heading	War Diary Of 32nd Divisional Ammunition Column, R.F.A. Period 1st To 28th February 1918. Volume 26		
War Diary	In the Field	11/02/1918	17/02/1918
Heading	32nd Divisional Artillery. 32nd Divisional Ammunition Column R.F.A. March 1918		
Heading	War Diary Of 32nd Divisional Ammunition Column R.F.A. Period 1st To 31st March 1918 Vol 27		
War Diary	In the Field	05/03/1918	30/03/1918
Heading	VI. Corps. Third Army. War Diary 32nd Divisional Ammunition Column, R.F.A. April 1918		
Heading	32nd Divisional Ammunition Column R.F.A. Period 1st To 30th April 1918. Vol 28		
War Diary	Field	03/04/1918	29/04/1918

Heading	War Diary 32nd Divisional Ammunition Column R.F.A. 1st To 31st May 1918		
War Diary	In the Field	05/05/1918	31/05/1918
Heading	War Diary 32nd Divisional Ammunition Column R.F.A. Period 1st June 1918 30th June 1918. Vol 30		
War Diary	In the Field	02/06/1918	26/06/1918
Heading	War Diary Of 32nd Divisional Ammunition Column R.F.A. From 1st July 1918 To 31st July 1918 Vol 31		
War Diary	In the Field	01/07/1918	30/07/1918
Heading	War Diary 32nd Divisional Ammunition Column R.F.A. Period 1st To 31st August 1918		
War Diary	In the Field	29/08/1918	30/08/1918
War Diary	In the Field	07/08/1918	29/08/1918
Heading	War Diary Of 32nd Divisional Ammunition Column R.F.A. Period:- 1st To 30th September 1918. Vol 33		
War Diary	In the Field	05/09/1918	30/09/1918
Heading	War Diary Of 32nd Divisional Ammunition Column R.F.A. From 1st October 1918 To 31st October 1918. Vol 34		
War Diary	In the Field	07/10/1918	31/10/1918
Heading	War Diary. Of 32nd Divisional Ammunition Column R.F.A. Period 1st To 30th November 1918. Vol 35		
War Diary	In the Field	02/11/1918	24/11/1918
Heading	War Diary. Of 32nd Divisional Ammunition Column R.F.A. Period 1st To 31st December 1918 Vol 36		
War Diary	In the Field	07/12/1918	28/12/1918
Heading	Lancashire Division (Late 32nd Divn) 32nd Divl Ammn Colmn Jan-Oct 1919		
Heading	War Diary. Of 32nd Divisional Ammunition Column R.F.A. Period. 1st To 31st January 1919. Vol 37		
War Diary	In the Field	10/01/1919	29/01/1919
Heading	War Diary. Of 32nd Divisional Ammunition Column R.F.A. Period 1st To 28th February 1919 Vol 38		
War Diary	Bonn Germany	02/02/1919	22/02/1919
Heading	War Diary. Of Lancashire (32nd) Divisional Ammunition Column RFA. Period 1st To 31st March 1919		
War Diary	Bonn Germany	01/03/1919	26/05/1919
War Diary	Bonn	18/06/1919	27/06/1919
War Diary	Bonn Germany.	21/07/1919	21/07/1919
War Diary	Bonn Germany.	20/07/1919	20/07/1919
War Diary	Bonn Germany.	10/08/1919	14/08/1919
War Diary		28/10/1919	28/10/1919

WO45/2381/2

32ND DIVISION DIVL ARTILLERY

32ND DIVL AMMN COLMN.

JAN 1916 - DEC 1918

1919 DEC

32nd Divisional Artillery.

Disembarked Havre 30.12.15.

32nd DIVISIONAL AMMUNITION COLUMN R.F.A.

JANUARY 1 9 1 6

Dec 1918

WAR DIARY

INTELLIGENCE SUMMARY

(Erase heading not required.)

Army Form C. 2118

Place	Date	Hour	Summary of Events and Information	Remarks and references to Appendices
	26-12-15	p.m.	Marched out of Sutton Mandeville Camp, near Salisbury in 5 parties	do.
	do	p.m.	Arrived at Southampton Docks, having entrained at Salisbury for Southampton in 8 trains - Column was complete in Officers & personnel and horses mules & vehicles.	do.
	28-12-15 / 29-12-15	mid-night	Embarked in the T.S.S. "Nirvana" and T.S.S. "Maidan".	do.
	29-12-15 "	5 p.m. 6 p.m.	T.S.S. "Maidan" sailed for Havre. T.S.S. "Nirvana" sailed for Havre.	do.
	30-12-15	a.m.	Arrived at Havre without incident :- (2/Lt. B.P. Luscombe removed to hospital in consequence of accident to foot sustained on journey to SALISBURY).	do.
	30-12-15 / 31-12-15		Column entrained at HALLE 3. HAVRE, & POINT 3. HAVRE, in 5 trains and detrained on	do.
	31-12-15		at LONGUEAU, near AMIENS. The Column proceeded by road through AMIENS to	do.
	1-1-16		ST. SAUVEUR (Somme) arriving on the 1st Jan. 1916.	
	4-1-16		Nos. 1 and 3 Sections marched by road to BAVELINCOURT (commune de Somme) halting for the night of the 4th at the Chateau at FRECHENCOURT.	do.
	5-1-16		Nos. 1 and 3 sections arrived at BAVELINCOURT and went into billets. (Note:- BAVELINCOURT at this time in occupation by 51st Div Amm Col.	do.

J. Walker Lt Col.

WAR DIARY
INTELLIGENCE SUMMARY
(Erase heading not required.)

Army Form C. 2118

Place	Date	Hour	Summary of Events and Information	Remarks and references to Appendices
	7-1-16	9 am 5 pm	Headquarters Staff and No. 2 Section proceeded by road from St. SAUVEUR to BAVELINCOURT arriving at 5 pm.	ts.
	7-1-16		On this day, this unit (32nd Div Amn Col.) took over the delivery of ammunition to the 32nd Division, from the 51st (Highland) Div Amm Col.	ts
	8-1-16		51st D.A.C. evacuated all billets etc and left BAVELINCOURT for ARGOEUVES (Somme), leaving BAVELINCOURT solely in occupation by 32nd Div. Amm. Col. Note:- Delivery and obtaining of Ammunition had commenced by this Unit on the 7th January 1916.	ts
	14-1-16		1 O.R. struck off - having been evacuated to C.C.S.	ts
	10-1-16		Commdg Officer of this Unit - Temty Major J Walker was this day gazetted Lieut-Colonel, whilst in command of this Unit.	ts
	21-1-16		3 O.R. taken on strength having arrived from HAVRE.	ts
	24-1-16		3 O.R. - do - - " - 161st Bde RFA.	ts
	24-1-16		2/Lieut. M.P. Robinson taken on strength having arrived from 2. Res. Bde. RFA. Preston.	ts.
	24-1-16		2 OR struck off strength - transfer to 161st Bde RFA - on authority of CRA 32nd Divnl. Artillery.	ts.

J Walker Lt Col.

32nd Divisional Artillery.

32nd DIVISIONAL AMMUNITION COLUMN R.F.A.

FEBRUARY 1 9 1 6

WAR DIARY / INTELLIGENCE SUMMARY

Army Form C. 2118

Place	Date	Hour	Summary of Events and Information	Remarks and references to Appendices
In the Field	6-2-16		Temp'y Capt. H. Green of this Unit temporarily attached to 108' Brigade Amm. Column RFA.	
"	15-2-16	11 am	Unit moved from BAVELINCOURT to BEAUCOURT SUR L'ANCRE (Province of Somme)	
	16-2-16		1 Bomdr. & 13 men, 3 G.S. wagons complete and 20 mules with harness transferred to 49" Divnl. Ammunition Column RFA (T) on instructions from Headquarters, 32nd Division - together with 176 rounds BX.	
	25-2-16		Capt. H. Green, above mentioned, struck off strength of this Unit, having been transferred to a 5th Division Unit. (Authority DAA & QMG X Corps No. 3852A. d/18-2-16)	
			During the last 3 days of the month, owing to severe frost and heavy snowfall, the Unit performed a considerable amount of Divisional Transport work, more than 50 G.S. wagons per day being engaged on this service, consequent on the withdrawal of heavy motor transport from the roads during the frost etc.	

Alfred Gray Lieut. Col.
Commdg. 32nd Div. Ammn. Col., R.F.A.

32nd Divisional Artillery.

32nd DIVISIONAL AMMUNITION COLUMN R.F.A.

MARCH 1 9 1 6

WAR DIARY

INTELLIGENCE SUMMARY

Army Form C. 2118

Place	Date	Hour	Summary of Events and Information	Remarks and references to Appendices
In the Field	2-3-16		Attachment. Capt. R.L. YATES temporarily attached to this Unit from 168th Brigade Ammn. Column RFA	
"	4-3-16	3 p.m.	Movt. The Unit evacuated billets in BEAUCOURT-SUR-HALLUE and moved to WARLOY-BAILLON (Somme)	
"	4-3-16		Duties. The commanding Officer took over the duties of Town Commandant of WARLOY-BAILLON and the Adjutant the duties of Town Major.	
"	10-3-16		Attachment. Lieut. D. MILLER temporarily attached to No. 1. Section of this Unit from 168th Bde Ammunition Column R.F.A.	
"	10-3-16		Transfer of Officer. 2/Lieut. W.P. ROBINSON transferred to 168th Brigade R.F.A.	
"	13-3-16		Officer - Removal. Sergt. R.L. YATES removed to England, having instructions to report to the War Office	
"	18-3-16		Equipment etc. - Transfer of - 3 hy. S. wagons, 18 mules and complete harness handed over to 49th Divisional Ammunition Column R.F.A.(T). (Authority C.R.A. 32nd Divn. M/372 d/16-3-16)	
"	30-3-16		Attachment. 2/Lieut. C.L.W. HAFFENDEN joined for attachment from 2.c. Res. Brigade R.F.A.	
"	31-3-16		Attachment. 2/Lieut. P.R. HAMILTON joined for attachment from BASE.	
"	31-3-16		Officer - Transfer. Lieut. D. MILLER transferred to 155th Brigade Ammunition Column RFA.	
"	31-3-16		General Remarks. A large number of wagons, averaging 35 per day, have been continuously engaged during the month in connection with Artillery and R.E. Services.	

James Walker Lieut. Col.
Commdg. 32nd. Div. Ammn. Col, R.F.A.

32nd Divisional Artillery.

32nd DIVISIONAL AMMUNITION COLUMN R. F.A.

APRIL 1 9 1 6

WAR DIARY

INTELLIGENCE SUMMARY

32 DAC Vol 4

Place	Date	Hour	Summary of Events and Information	Remarks and references to Appendices
In the Field	1916 8. Apl		2nd Lieut. C. L. N. HAFFENDEN transferred from this Unit to 164th Brigade R.F.A.	fo.
"	10 "		2nd Lieut. O.D. YENDALL joined this Unit on transfer from 164th Brigade RFA	fo.
"	28 "		66 N.C.O's and men detached from this Unit to form V/32 Heavy Trench Mortar Bty.	fo.

James Walker, Lieut. Col.
Commdg. 32nd. Div. Ammn. Col., R.F.A.

32nd Divisional Artillery.

32nd DIVISIONAL AMMUNITION COLUMN R.F.A.

M A Y   1 9 1 6

WAR DIARY or INTELLIGENCE SUMMARY

Army Form C. 2118

(Erase heading not required.)

Place	Date	Hour	Summary of Events and Information	Remarks and references to Appendices
In the Field			**Promotions:** Temp. Lieut. G.E.F. HARLEY, promoted temporary Captain with effect from March 8th 1916. (London Gazette dated 25th April 1916)	
			Temporary 2/Lieut. C.E. JOHNSON } Promoted Temporary Lieutenants (London Gazette 25th April 1916)	
			Temporary 2/Lieut. B. MONK }	
"	20.5.16		**Town Major** The Adjutant relinquished the duties of Town Major of WARLOY-BAILLON on this date.	
"	26.5.16		**Reorganization** In consequence of the Re-establishment of Divisional Artillery, this Unit was on this date reorganized into Headquarters and 4 Sections (forming "A" and "B" Echelons) and the following transfers to this Unit were effected:-	
			Lieut. H.C. WORRALL from 164th Brigade Amm. Column	
			2/Lt. W. SANDS " 161st " " "	
			2/Lt. A. ISHERWOOD " 164th " " "	
			2/Lt. A.B. HEINEMANN " 161st Brigade	
			93 N.C.O's and men were taken on the strength from 153rd Brigade R.F.A.	
			83 " " " " " " " 161st " "	
			71 " " " " " " " 164th " "	
			60 " " " " " " " 164th " "	
			Total 287	
			The following horses and mules also were taken on the strength from the Units mentioned:-	

J. Hicks Lieut. Col.
Commdg. 32nd Div. Ammn. Col, R.F.A. (continue p 2)

WAR DIARY
or
INTELLIGENCE SUMMARY

Army Form C. 2118

Place	Date	Hour	Summary of Events and Information	Remarks and references to Appendices
	26-5-16		Reorganization (continued)	
			From 155th Brigade RFA — 100 horses	
			" 161st " " 118 " and 41 mules	
			" 164 " " 66 "	
			" 168 " " 31 " 24 "	
			315 horses and 65 mules	
			In addition to the foregoing, the necessary vehicles, harness and stores were taken over from the Brigade Ammunition Columns mentioned, to complete this Unit to establishment and 16 G.S. wagons being their surplus in this Unit, were evacuated to Advanced H.T. Base.	

J. Walker Lieut. Col.
Commdg. 32nd. Div. Ammn. Col., R.F.A.

32nd Divisional Artillery.

32nd DIVISIONAL AMMUNITION COLUMN R.F.A.

JUNE 1916

32 June
Army Form C. 2118
2nd Div
Amm Col

WAR DIARY
~~INTELLIGENCE SUMMARY~~
(Erase heading not required.)

DIVISIONAL AMMUNITION COLUMN
No. ...... JUNE
Date 1
2nd ...... R.F.A.

Instructions regarding War Diaries and Intelligence Summaries are contained in F.S. Regs., Part II. and the Staff Manual respectively. Title Pages will be prepared in manuscript.

Place	Date	Hour	Summary of Events and Information	Remarks and references to Appendices
In the field	3.6.16		DECORATIONS- ETC. The Commanding Officer of this Unit, Lieut-Col. J. Walker, had conferred upon him the D.S.O. Notification of this appeared in the London Gazette of this date. Amongst the list of Officers mentioned in despatches from Genl. D. Haig, of Col 30th, received by the War Office on 15th June 1916, Lt-Col Walker's name appeared.	VCB W:
-do-	5.6.16		JOININGS OF OFFICERS. Lieut F.W. Tobutt, taken on the strength from Advanced H.T. Base, Abbeville. 2/Lieut A.B. Heinemann, taken on the strength from 161st Brigade R.F.A.	/s.
-do-	5.6.16		OFFICERS-ADMISSION TO HOSPITAL. 2/Lieut F.W. de Valda admitted to Hospital sick, and was subsequently evacuated to Base.	
-do-	6.6.16		ACT OF COURAGE. No L/13900, A/Bdr. W. Robinson, of this Unit was mentioned in Fourth Army Routine Orders of this date, in connection with an appreciation of his services in stopping runaway horses attached to a G.S. wagon, at Warloy-Baillon (Somme) on the 21st May 1916.	/s.
-do-	12.6.16		ATTACHMENTS. 1 Officer, 31 N.C.O.'s and men, 47 animals and transport of the HQ 1st Div. Amm. Col. (T) were attached to this Unit for duty until 28.6.16.	/s.
-do-	14.6.16		TIME. The time was advanced 60 minutes at 11pm on this day in accordance with G.R.O.	/s.

1875 Wt. W593/826 1,000,000 4/15 J.B.C. & A. A.D.S.S./Forms/C. 2118.

WAR DIARY or INTELLIGENCE SUMMARY

Army Form C. 2118

Place	Date	Hour	Summary of Events and Information	Remarks and references to Appendices
In the Field	18.6.16		**CASUALTIES.** The first casualty in the Unit occurred on this date, when No. 25692 Driver W. LISLE was shot through the leg by hostile M.G. fire whilst with a convoy delivering ammunition near to the firing line. Two more minor casualties occurred from shrapnel, the next day, neither of which necessitated admission to hospital.	/D.
-Do-	25.6.16		**ATTACHMENTS.** No 1 Section of the H.Q. D.A.C.(T) combat, comprising 3 Officers + 166 N.C.O.'s and men, together with animals and transport were attached to this Unit for duty, on this date.	/D.
-Do-	30.6.16		**JOININGS OF OFFICERS.** 2/Lieut. E.A. RYRIE and 2/Lieut. F.H. LEMON joined from Base for temporary attachment	/D.
-Do-	1.6.16 to 19.6.16		**AMMUNITION DUMPING.** In preparation for the present offensive operations, this Unit delivered from a Divisional Dump established at WARLOY-BAILLON, to twenty-three Battery positions, and to various Infantry and Artillery Magazines, the following ammunition. The figures given are approximate.	/D.

A	AX	BX	S.A.A. 303	2" T.M.	3" T.M.	240m/m T.M.	GRENADES No 5
43,500	9,800	13,350	3,270,000	11,400	16,150	114	60,700
			GRENADES No 19			GRENADES No 20	
			300			6000	

WAR DIARY or INTELLIGENCE SUMMARY

Army Form C. 2118

(Erase heading not required.)

Place	Date	Hour	Summary of Events and Information	Remarks and references to Appendices
In the Field	7-6-16 to 19-6-16		**AMMUNITION DUMPING** (Cont.) In addition to the above, the Column delivered from a light railway in close proximity to the firing line, the following ammunition to various battery positions $\dfrac{A}{12800}$ $\dfrac{AX}{6400}$ $\dfrac{BX}{3600}$ All the above ammunition dumping was carried out between the 7th and 19th of June, the work being performed principally at night.	

T. Walker. Lieut. Col.
Commdg. 32nd. Div. Ammn. Col., R.F.A.

[Stamp: 32ND DIVISIONAL AMMUNITION COLUMN * R.F.A. * No..... Date JUNE 3]

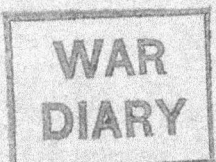

DIVISIONAL AMMUNITION COLUMN, R.F.A.

32nd DIVISION.

J U L Y

1 9 1 6

WAR DIARY
INTELLIGENCE SUMMARY

Army Form C. 2118

(Erase heading not required.)

Instructions regarding War Diaries and Intelligence Summaries are contained in F.S. Regs., Part II. and the Staff Manual respectively. Title Pages will be prepared in manuscript.

Place	Date	Hour	Summary of Events and Information	Remarks and references to Appendices
In the Field	1/7/16		OFFICERS POSTINGS. 2/Lieut E.A. Ryrie) from Base to this unit with effect from 30/6/16. 2/Lieut F.H. Lemon)	
-do-	1/7/16		2/Lieut F.W. de Valda struck off the strength with effect from 26/6/16, having been evacuated to England, sick.	
-do-	3/7/16		2/Lieut E.A. Ryrie posted to "A" Batt. 164th Bde R.F.A.	
-do-	6/7/16		2/Lieut W. Sands posted to 161st Bde. R.F.A.	
-do-	7/7/16		Captain R.E. Grice Hutchinson, C. of E. Chaplain attached	
-do-	7/7/16		2/Lieut F.H. Lemon posted to 155th Bde. R.F.A.	
-do-	14/7/16		DETACHMENT, 49th D.A.C. No 1 Section of the 49th D.A.C. (T), attached to this unit, was returned to its own formation.	
-do-	17/7/16		MOVE OF DETACHMENT The S.A.A. and Grenade portions of this unit, comprising 5 Officers, 224 N.C.O's and men, with 55 vehicles, 138 horses and 182 mules moved from WARLOY-BAILLON (Somme) to AMPLIER (East of DOULLENS), on this date.	
-do-	17/7/16		OFFICERS POSTINGS. 2/Lieut E.N. Crew) taken on the strength from Base. 2/Lieut R.C. Knowles)	
-do-	19/7/16	11 a.m.	MOVE OF UNIT. On the withdrawal of the 32nd Division from the SOMME Area, this unit evacuated billets etc. at WARLOY-BAILLON (Somme) on this day and marched to AUTHIEULE, (East of DOULLENS), arriving at 5 p.m. and camped in bivouacs.	
-do-	20/7/16	6 a.m.	The unit moved out of AUTHIEULE and continued march to AUBROMETZ (Refce 3. c.) arriving here at 12.30 p.m. and camped in bivouacs.	
-do-	21/7/16	9 a.m.	The unit moved out of AUBROMETZ and continued march to EPS (Refce. 1. d) arriving here at 3.30 p.m. and camped in bivouacs.	
-do-	22/7/16	10 a.m.	The unit moved out of EPS and continued march to NEDON (Refce Map "HAZEBROUCK Sheet 5-a" E.6.) and camped in bivouacs.	Refce. Map LENS Sheet 11 1/100000

WAR DIARY or INTELLIGENCE SUMMARY

Army Form C. 2118

(Erase heading not required.)

Place	Date	Hour	Summary of Events and Information	Remarks and references to Appendices
In the Field	24/7/16		DETACHMENT. The detachment of the unit mentioned previously, rejoined the Column at NEDON on this date from ECQUEDECQUES, near LILLERS.	
-do-	28/7/16		JOININGS OF OFFICERS. Captain H. Whittles joined from "C" Batt. 168th Bde R.F.A., having been posted to this unit by H.Q. 32nd Divisional Artillery.	
-do-	29/7/16		MOVE OF UNIT. The unit moved out of NEDON and marched to LABEUVRIERE, (West of BETHUNE), and went into billets and bivouacs at this village.	
-do-	1/7/16 to 17/7/16		AMMUNITION SUPPLY. During the bombardment and subsequent offensive operations by the Fourth Army in the Somme area, the unit continued to supply large quantities of ammunition to the Division. Approximate figures of gun ammunition supplied during period 1st to 17th July, are as follows:-	

```
18 pr Shrap    18 pr H.E.    4.5 H.E.
   63750         22250        16100
```

In addition a supply of Infantry ammunition was maintained during the period.

J. ????
Lieut. Col.
Commdg. 32nd. Div. Ammn. Col., R.F.A.

32nd Divisional Artillery.

32nd DIVISIONAL AMMUNITION COLUMN R.F.A.

AUGUST 1 9 1 6

Army Form C. 2118

WAR DIARY
INTELLIGENCE SUMMARY
(Erase heading not required.)

AUGUST 1916.

32nd D.C. DIVISIONAL AMMUNITION COLUMN No........ Date........ R.F.A.

Instructions regarding War Diaries and Intelligence Summaries are contained in F. S. Regs., Part II. and the Staff Manual respectively. Title Pages will be prepared in manuscript.

Place	Date	Hour		Summary of Events and Information	Remarks and references to Appendices
In the Field	5/8/16		MOVE OF UNIT.	The unit complete moved from LABEUVRIERE to BETHUNE (Ref. E. 11 b 5.5. Bethune Combined Sheet) and recommenced ammunition supply to the 32nd Division which had gone into the line.	/s/
In the Field	7/8/16		OFFICERS.	2/Lieut (late Tempy Captain) E. WHITTIES posted to the 40th Divisional Artillery	/s/
In the Field	7/8/16		CASUALTIES.	As the result of a hostile bombardment of BETHUNE, the Adjutant of the unit, Lieut C.G. TOOGOOD became ill, suffering from shell shock and was removed to hospital the next day, subsequently being evacuated to England on the 15th August. 2/Lieut I.O.R. was also injured in the leg by a shell splinter and admitted to hospital.	/s/
In the Field -do-	11/8/16 12/8/16		MOVE. MOVE.	"B" Echelon of the unit moved to ANNEZIN. (Ref. Bethune Combined Sheet E.S.b.) "A" Echelon of the unit moved to ANNEZIN.	/s/
In the Field	17/8/16		CASUALTY.	No 14901, Driver HUNSLEY H. died in hospital as the result of injuries sustained from a kick by a mule on the 12th August.	/s/
In the Field	22/8/16		APPOINTMENT.	The Officer Commanding the unit was appointed Town Major, ANNEZIN.	/s/
In the Field	28/8/16		OFFICERS.	2/Lieut R.C. KNOWLES and 2/Lieut E.N. CREW posted to 1st Division, 3rd Corps.	/s/
			GENERAL.	Owing to Ammunition Sub Parks ceasing to deliver ammunition to D.A.C's, in order to conserve petrol, this unit, from the 12th instant has drawn all ammunition for the 32nd Division from Railhead, using its own transport.	/s/

J. Walker. Lieut. Col.
Commdg. 32nd. Div. Ammn. Col., R.F.A.

32nd Divisional Artillery

/"

32nd DIVISIONAL AMMUNITION COLUMN R.F.A.

SEPTEMBER 1 9 1 6

Army Form C. 2118

WAR DIARY or INTELLIGENCE SUMMARY

(Erase heading not required.)

Instructions regarding War Diaries and Intelligence Summaries are contained in F. S. Regs., Part II. and the Staff Manual respectively. Title Pages will be prepared in manuscript.

Place	Date	Hour	Summary of Events and Information	Remarks and references to Appendices
In the Field.	6-9-16		2/Lieut. Yewdall admitted to hospital sick. Discharged 16-9-16.	
	11-9-16.		Lieut. F.W.Tobutt of this Unit, was arrested on this date on a charge of Drunkenness.—Trial by G.C.M. was subsequently fixed for 1st. October 1916.	
	15-9-16.		2/Lieut. F.H.Hirst attached to this Unit from Base, until 17th. September 1916.	
	16-9-16.		Lieut. F.W.Wisher attached to this Unit from 2/32 T.M.Battery.	
	19-9-16.		Consequent upon the Reorganisation of the Divisional Artillery, all surplus W.O.s., N.C.O.s, and men from the various Artillery Brigades, were posted to this Unit pending their dispatch to the Base, and on this date, and during the next few days, 66 W.O.s, N.C.O.s, and men were attached to this Unit, and still remain attached.	
	19-9-16.		2/Lieut. C.L.Paul posted to this Unit from 155 Brigade. R.F.A.	
			2/Lieut. G.W.Giles posted to this Unit from 164 Brigade. R.F.A.	
	24-9-16.		The Officer Commanding this Unit handed over the duties of Town Major of ANNEZIN-les-BETHUNE to Lieut. Davidson of the 11th. Border Regiment.	
	28-9-16.		2/Lieut. G.Fotherby posted to this Unit from 164 Brigade.R.F.A.	

Walker Lieut. Col.
Comndg. 82nd. Div. Ammn. Col., R.F.A.

32nd Divisional Artillery.

32nd DIVISIONAL AMMUNITION COLUMN R.F.A.

OCTOBER 1 9 1 6

WAR DIARY
INTELLIGENCE SUMMARY
(Erase heading not required.)

Army Form C. 2118

Place	Date	Hour	Summary of Events and Information	Remarks and references to Appendices
IN THE FIELD	1-10-16		OFFICERS. G.C.M. Temp/y Lieut. F.W. TOBUTT, of this unit was to-day tried by G.C.M. on a charge of drunkenness. Sentence promulgated on 13.10.16. Accused was found guilty and sentenced to be dismissed from the service. He was evacuated to England on 14.10.16.	/s/
"	9.10.16		ARTILLERY - REORGANIZATION. The surplus personnel attached to this unit, consequent on the reorganization of the Divisional Artillery, numbering 55. O.R. in all, were this day despatched to R.34 R.F.A. Base.	/s/
"	10.10.16		At an inspection of horse standings, etc of this Division this day, by Major-Genl Rycroft, G.O.C. 32nd Division, the prize for the best improved Harness shelter was awarded to No 2 Section of this unit.	/s/
"	16.10.16		MOVES. In consequence of the move of 32nd Division from First Army area to Reserve Army area, this unit commenced to move on this day - from ANNEZIN-LEZ-BETHUNE to LABEUVRIERE (East of BETHUNE).	/s/
"	17.10.16		Unit moved from LABEUVRIERE to MONCHY-BRETON (Ref. F.2 Lino Sheet 1/100000. 10.11)	/s/
"	18.10.16		" " " MONCHY-BRETON to REBREUVE-LACOUTURE (" E.3 -do-)	
"	19.10.16		" " " REBREUVE-LACOUTURE to GEZAINCOURT (" D.5 -do-)	
"	20.10.16		" " " GEZAINCOURT and occupied bivouacs on the road between SARTON and THIÈVRES. (REF. F.5. Lino Sheet 1/100000. 10.11)	

WAR DIARY or INTELLIGENCE SUMMARY

Army Form C. 2118

Place	Date	Hour	Summary of Events and Information	Remarks and references to Appendices
In the Field	23.10.16		AMMUNITION DUMP :- This unit furnished a party of 1 Officer + 45 N.C.O.s + men to work a large ammunition dump for the 51st Division at MAILLY - MAILLET; also a party of 21 O.R. for the 3rd Division dump at ACHEUX. 	JW
"	24.9.16			
"	29.10.16		OFFICERS :- Tempy 2/Lieut F. WISHER, M.C. attached to this unit, relinquished the temporary rank of Lieut on ceasing to command Z.32 T.M. Battery.	JW

James Walker Lieut. Col.
Commdg. 32nd. Div. Ammn. Coln., R.F.A.

32nd Divisional Artillery.

32nd DIVISIONAL AMMUNITION COLUMN R.F.A.

NOVEMBER 1 9 1 6

WAR DIARY

Army Form C. 2118

Place	Date	Hour	Summary of Events and Information	Remarks and references to Appendices
In the Field	2.11.16		**Ammunition Dumps:** 3 Corporals of this unit proceeded to take charge of 3 Infantry Dumps in the front line on this date.	To H.Col.
"	16.11.16		**Officer.** 2nd Lieut. T. LITTLEWOOD, reported from Base and is temporarily attached to this Unit from this date.	To H.Col.
"	28.11.16		2nd Lieut. A. ISHERWOOD was admitted to hospital on this date.	To Col.
"	18.11.16		**Detachments etc.** The Small Arm Section of this unit comprising 3 Officers, 200 O.R.s, 288 animals & 49 vehicles, was detached for duty at P.17 a 5.2 (Ref. Sheet 57 D. 1/40,000), on this date.	To I.Col.
"	23.11.16		The parties at MAILLY-MAILLET (51st Div. Dump) (1 officer, 45 O.R.s) and ACHEUX (3rd Div. Dump), (21. O.R) were attached on this date to the 2nd Division A.R.P. at P.2.b.9.3. (Ref 57 D. 1/40,000)	
"	30.11.16		**General.** The unit is still in bivouacs, as reported in War Diary of October.	

J Walker
Lieut. Col.
Commdg. 32nd. Div. Ammn. Col., R.F.A.

WAR DIARY

DECEMBER, 1916.

(Erase heading not required.)

Instructions regarding War Diaries and Intelligence Summaries are contained in F.S. Regs., Part II. and the Staff Manual respectively. Title Pages will be prepared in manuscript.

Army Form C. 2118

Place	Date	Hour	Summary of Events and Information	Remarks and references to Appendices
THIEVRES to ST. OUEN	6-12-16.		MOVE. On the withdrawal of the 52nd. Division into rest, this Unit moved from THIEVRES to ST. OUEN (Reference LENS Sheet 11 - approx: B.6.) and commenced building Standings etc.	/s/
	5-12-16.		OFFICERS. 2/Lieut. A.I.Sherwood struck off the strength of Unit - evacuated to England, sick.	/s/
	6-12-16.		Lieut. W.L.Scott. R.F.A., temporarily attached to this Unit from Base, and reposted to 168 Bde. R.F.A. on 7-12-16.	/s/
	10-12-16.		Lieut. C.G.Toogood R.F.A., re-joined this Unit from Base.	/s/
	13-12-16.		Lieut. and A/Adjt. J.E.Johnson appointed Adjutant of this Unit with effect from 8-8-16. (Authority: V Corps. V.A. 278/22 of 13-12-16.)	/s/
	16-12-16.		DETACHMENT. A party of 2 Officers and 93 Other Ranks, with vehicles and transport were attached to 161st. Bde. R.F.A. from this Unit for the purpose of assisting to construct standings etc. This party returned on the 30th. Decr. 1916.	/s/
	20-12-16.		INSPECTION. A Section of this Unit, along with various Batteries of 52nd. Divl. Artillery were inspected by Lieut. General Fanshawe, and received a favourable report.	/s/
	29-12-16.		INSPECTION. This Unit, with the remainder of the 32nd. Divl. Artillery was inspected by G.O.C., 32nd. Division at a march past, and received a very favourable report.	/s/

James Walker Lieut. Col.
Commdg. 32nd. Div. Ammn. Col, R.F.A.

"Confidential"

War Diary

32nd Divisional Ammunition Column R.F.A.

From 1st to 31st January 1917.

WAR DIARY

32nd Divisional Ammunition Column, R.F.A.

JANUARY 1917.

Army Form C. 2118

(Erase heading not required.)

Place	Date	Hour	Summary of Events and Information	Remarks and references to Appendices
In the Field.	1917 Jan. 4th		OFFICERS. 2/Lieut B.W. GILES posted to B Battery, 155th Bde, R.F.A. - Returned to this Unit on 24.1.17.	1/5
-do-	-do-		DETACHMENT. 1 Officer and 50 men from this unit were attached to the 7th D.A.C. R.F.A. for duties on an ammunition dump, until the 21st January 1917.	1/5
-do-	Jan.7th		OFFICERS. 2/Lieut W. SANDS, taken on the strength of this unit from F. Battery, 161st Bde, R.F.A.	1/6
-do-	Jan. 15th		MOVE. This unit moved from ST OUEN (Somme) on this day as follows. No 1 Section) To camp on the BUS-BERTRANCOURT Road. "B" Echelon) Refce. J. 26. France 57 d. H.Q. Staff) No 2 Section) To ORVILLE. Refce. H.4. France 57 d. No 3 Section)	1/6 1/6
-do-	Jan. 15th		AMMUNITION DUMPS. The ammunition dumps of the 3rd Division and one of the 7th Division were taken over by this unit.	1/6
-do-	Jan. 21st		Officers. 2/Lieut W.D LITTLEWOOD admitted to hospital, sick.	1/6
-do-	Jan. 23rd.		REORGANIZATION. On this date this unit was reorganized as follows. No 1 Section - Remained unchanged. No 3 Section - Became No 2 Section of "A" Echelon, 32nd D.A.C. No 4 Section ("B" Echelon) remained "B" Echelon. No 2 Section became 155th Army Field Artillery Brigade Ammunition Column. The necessary transfers consequent on this reorganization were duly carried out, and O.C. 155th Army Field Artillery Brigade. took over command of the 155th A.F.A. B.A.C. on 31st January 1917.	1/6
-do-	-do-		OFFICERS. Capt. H.C. WORRALL, 2/Lieut C.I. PAUL, 2/Lieut W. SANDS and 2/Lieut W.D. LITTLEWOOD. were transferred along with No 2 Section of this unit to 155th A.F.A. B.A.C.	1/6

WAR DIARY 32nd Divisional Ammunition Column, R.F.A. Army Form C. 2118

or

INTELLIGENCE SUMMARY JANUARY 1917. (Sheet 2)

(Erase heading not required.)

Place	Date	Hour	Summary of Events and Information	Remarks and references to Appendices
In the Field.	Jan.31st		MOVE. H.Q. Staff of this unit moved from ORVILLE to BUS les ARTOIS. (Refce. J. 26. France 57 d)	/5 /8
	Jan.29th		3 Officers and 30 other ranks from the 62nd Divisional Artillery were attached to this unit for instruction in the method of managing Ammunition Dumps.	

J. Walker Lieut. Col.
Commdg. 32nd. Div. Ammn. Col., R.F.A.

Confidential War Diary

of:

32nd Divisional Ammunition Column, R.F.A.

Vol. 14

From: 1st February 1917
To: 28th February 1917

WAR DIARY
or
INTELLIGENCE SUMMARY

Army Form C. 2118

(Erase heading not required.)

FEBRUARY 1917

Place	Date	Hour	Summary of Events and Information	Remarks and references to Appendices
In the Field.	1/2/17 to 18/2/17		**AMMUNITION DUMPS.** This unit was engaged constructing and managing various Dumps in the V Corps area, for Gun ammunition, Grenades etc. In all; 7 ammunition dumps were being worked or under construction by this unit.	
-do-	18/2/17		The ammunition dumps etc. were handed over to the 19th and 52nd Divisions.	
-do-	19/2/17		**MOVE OF UNIT.** The unit moved from BUS LES ARTOIS (No 2 Section from ORVILLE) to NAOURS 8 miles North of AMIENS.	
-do-	23/2/17		The unit moved to ARGOEUVES (Ref. AMIENS Sheet 1/100000 G. 1.	
-do-	24/2/17		The unit moved to DOMART sur la LUCE (Ref. France Sheet 66 E. c. 3. a.)	
-do-	25/2/17		The unit moved to MEZIERES (Ref. France Sheet 66 F. D. 26 a) and re-commenced ammunition supply to the 32nd Division.	

J. Walker, Lieut. Col.
Commdg. 32nd. Div. Ammn. Col., R.F.A.

Vol 15

CONFIDENTIAL

32ND
DIVISIONAL AMMUNITION COLUMN
R.F.A.

WAR DIARY

From: March 1st 1917
To: March 31st 1917

Army Form C. 2118.

WAR DIARY
or
INTELLIGENCE-SUMMARY.
(Erase heading not required.)

Place	Date	Hour	Summary of Events and Information	Remarks and references to Appendices
In the Field	1917 Mar 3rd		DUMP FOR AMMUNITION. A new gun ammunition dump was established at LE QUESNEL, Refce. K.8.c.3.3 and was run by this unit as well as a dump for Infantry ammunition at the same place.	/5 Mar
-do-	Mar 18th		MOVE. On retreat of the enemy this unit moved from MEZIERES. (Ref.D.26.a.9.9.) to the RAPERIE (Ref. K.22.b.1.1) Refuce REF W.E	/s
-do-	Mar 19th		On this date the unit moved from the RAPERIE to ETALON (Ref. H.15.a. 66 D)	/s
-do-	Mar 20th		On this date the unit moved from ETALON to CURCHY (Ref. H.5.c. 66 D.)	/s
-do-	Mar 20th		BRIDGE. This unit bridged the River d'INGON at CURCHY. (Ref. H.9.a.8.9.) 66D. The bridge was tested by a R.E. Officer and found capable of carrying 8 tons on one axle. The bridge was named WALKER'S BRIDGE and a notice to that effect erected.	/s
-do-	March 23rd		MOVE. The S.A. Section of this unit moved from CURCHY to NESLE (Ref. I.19.a. 66 D) and established a dump there for Infantry ammunition.	/s
-do-	March 24th		TIME. Summer time was taken up by this unit and time advanced by 1 hour.	/s
-do- -do- -do-	MARCH 28th MARCH 30		MOVE. Headquarters and "A" Echelon of this unit moved from CURCHY to BUNY (Ref. J.7.b.66 D) "B" Echelon of this unit moved from CURCHY to TOULLE (Ref. J.5.c. 66 D) "B" Echelon of this unit moved from TOULLE to OFFOY (Ref. J.15.c. 66 D)	/s /s /s
-do-	MARCH 31st		No 2 Section, 35th D.A.C. were attached to this unit on this date, and subsequently a portion of "B" Echelon, 35th D.A.C. were attached.	/s
-do-	MARCH 30		Headquarters and "A" Echelon of this unit moved from BUNY to DOUILLY (Ref.E.25.b. 66 D)	/s

Army Form C. 2118.

WAR DIARY
or
INTELLIGENCE SUMMARY.

(Erase heading not required.)

Place	Date	Hour	Summary of Events and Information	Remarks and references to Appendices
In the Field	March 31st.		**DUMPS.** Dumps were established by this unit for Artillery ammunition at DOUCHY (Ref. F.19.c. 66 D) and GERMAINE (Ref. E.7.b. 66 D) and a considerable amount of ammunition was brought up from the rear.	A/T B/-
	March 31st.		An Infantry dump was established at FORESTE. (Ref. E.15.a. 66 D)	

J. Walker Lieut. Col.
Commdg. 32nd. Div. Ammn. Col, R.F.A.

Confidential

War Diary

— : of : —

32nd Divisional Ammunition Column,
R.F.A.

From: 1st April 1917.
To: 30th April 1917.

Army Form C. 2118.

Instructions regarding War Diaries and Intelligence Summaries are contained in F. S. Regs., Part II. and the Staff Manual respectively. Title pages will be prepared in manuscript.

WAR DIARY
or
INTELLIGENCE SUMMARY. APRIL 1917.

(Erase heading not required.)

SHEET. 1

Place	Date April.	Hour	Summary of Events and Information		Remarks and references to Appendices
In the Field.	1		ATTACHMENTS.	No 2 Section and a portion of "B" Echelon of 35th D.A.C. were attached to this unit, in connection with ammunition supply of 159th Bde, R.F.A. attached to 32nd Divisional Artillery from 35th Divisional Artillery.	/a/
-do-	2			8. Other ranks reinforcements joined this unit from Base and were subsequently posted to Batteries of 32nd Divisional Artillery.	/b/
-do-	3		MOVE.	"B" Echelon of this unit moved from OFFOY (Ref. J.15.c. Sheet 66d) to DOUILLY (Ref. E.25.b, Sheet 66d), where it joined the remainder of the Column.	/c/
-do-	4		AMMUNITION DUMP.	A large dump for Field Artillery and 60 pr ammunition was formed at DOUILLY and managed by this unit.	/d/
-do-	5		MOVE.	"A" Echelon of this unit and No 2 Section, 35th D.A.C. moved forward to VAUX (Ref.F.1.d. Sheet 66d) and ETREILLERS (Ref. X.27.c., Sheet 62c) and took over the supply and delivery of ammunition direct to Battery positions of 32nd Divisional Artillery, owing to the wagon lines of the Batteries having been ordered by the C.R.A. to give their horses rest.	
-do-	8			27 other ranks reinforcements joined this unit from Base and were subsequently posted to Batteries of the 32nd Divisional Artillery.	/e/
-do-	10			2/Lieut C.J. HORNSBY was taken on the strength from Base on this date.	/f/
-do-	12		MOVE OF DETACHMENT.	The portion of "B" Echelon, 35th D.A.C. attached to this unit, rejoined its own unit on this date.	/g/
-do-	15		OFFICERS...	Lieut C.G. TOOGOOD was struck off the strength of this unit, having been appointed a Deputy Assistant Director of Forestry.	/h/
-do-	16			21. other ranks reinforcements joined this unit from Base and were subsequently posted to Batteries of 32nd Divisional Artillery.	/i/
-do-	21			57 other ranks reinforcements joined this unit from Base and were subsequently posted to Batteries of the 32nd Divisional Artillery.	/j/

Army Form C. 2118.

SHEET 2.
WAR DIARY
or
INTELLIGENCE SUMMARY.
(Erase heading not required.)

Instructions regarding War Diaries and Intelligence Summaries are contained in F. S. Regs., Part II. and the Staff Manual respectively. Title pages will be prepared in manuscript.

[Stamp: 32nd DIVISIONAL AMMUNITION COLUMN, No....., APRIL 1917, R.F.A.]

Place	Date	Hour	Summary of Events and Information	Remarks and references to Appendices
In the Field	April 21		**ADMINISTRATION.** This unit along with the remainder of the 32nd Divisional Artillery came under the orders of the 61st Division which had relieved the 32nd Division; less Artillery.	
-do-	22		**OFFICERS.** 2/Lieut B.W. GILES of this unit was transferred to IV Corps Ammunition Parks on this date.	
-do-	25		2/Lieut A.B. HEINEMANN was struck off the strength of this unit having been invalided to England.	
-do-	30		2/Lieut E.J. SHOTT was taken on the strength from Base on this date.	
-do-	30		**ASSISTANCE TO CIVILIANS.** This unit supplied men and animals to assist French civilians in ploughing land retaken from the enemy.	

			AMMUNITION. During the month this D.A.C. has received:—
			     18 pr Shrapnel 58417 rds
			     18 pr H.E. 21509 "
			     4.5 How. Ammtn. 23737 "
			 and has issued to Batteries:—
			     18 pr Shrapnel 38744 rds
			     18 pr H.E. 15730 "
			     4.5 How. Ammtn. 18550 "	

			STRENGTH. At the beginning of the month:— 15 Officers, 675 other ranks. At the end of the month:— 14 Officers, 692 other ranks.	

J. Walker, Lieut. Col.
Commdg. 32nd. Div. Ammn. Col., R.F.A.

Confidential

War Diary
—: of :—
32nd Divisional Ammunition Column, R.F.A.

From :- 1st May 1917
To :- 31st May 1917

Army Form C. 2118.

WAR DIARY
or
INTELLIGENCE SUMMARY.
(Erase heading not required.)

May 1917

Place	Date	Hour	Summary of Events and Information	Remarks and references to Appendices
In the Field	1st to 3rd May		**Assistance to Civilians.** The unit continued to render assistance to French civilians by supplying horses and men to plough fields in the re-occupied area.	
-do-	4th		**Inspection.** The whole Column was inspected by the G.O.C, 32nd Division and B.G. R.A 32nd Division. Satisfaction was expressed in regard to the condition of the animals.	
-do-	5th		**Officers.** 2nd Lieut. P.H.THOMPSON. was taken on the strength from 16/3/. Brigade, R.F.A.	
-do-	6th		**Attachments etc.** No.2 Section, 35th D.A.C. rejoined their own unit on this date, after being attached to this unit. No.1 Section 61st D.A.C. attached to this unit with effect from this date.	
-do-	11th		**Officers.** Major J.K.LOCKHART, attached to this unit from 161st Bde. R.F.A.	
-do-	12th		Lines of No.1 Section of this unit lightly shelled by enemy - 1 ammunition wagon damaged - 1 mule killed	
-do-	14th		Lines of No.1 Section of this unit lightly shelled by enemy - no casualties.	

32ND DIVISIONAL AMMUNITION COLUMN
No.
R.F.A.

Army Form C. 2118.

WAR DIARY
or
INTELLIGENCE SUMMARY.

(Erase heading not required.)

May 1917

32ND DIVISIONAL AMMUNITION COLUMN
R.F.A.

Place	Date	Hour	Summary of Events and Information	Remarks and references to Appendices
In the Field	14		**Move.** No 2 section of this unit moved with No 1st Brigade, R.H.A to ETAPLES – 15th inst to FOLIES – 16 inst to MORISEL (Refer France Sheets 66D and 66E)	
	15		**Officers.** 2 Lieut H.D. BOYD (T). Taken on the strength from 63rd Divl. Artillery.	
	16		**Move.** No 1 Section of this unit moved from VAUX to DOUILLY (Ref. France. Sheet 66D).	
	17		No 1 Section, 63rd D.A.C. rejoined their own unit.	
	18		**Ammunition.** This unit cleared 32nd Division area of ammunition (including dump of approximately 35000 rounds), on the taking over of the sector by the French.	
	19		**Move.** This unit, less No 2 Section moved to FOLIES (Refer France. Sheet 66E).	
	20		The whole unit moved to DEMUIN (Refer France Sheet 66E).	
	22		**Officers.** 2nd Lieut H.D. BOYD admitted to hospital on this date.	
	23		**Move.** This unit entrained along with remainder of 32nd Divisional Artillery at MARCELCAVE and GUILLACOURT (Refer France Sheet 66E) and detrained at CAESTRE.	
	24		The unit moved to outskirts of BAILLEUL (Ref. Hazebrouck Sheet 5A–I–4) and encamped in bivouacs.	

Army Form C. 2118.

WAR DIARY
or
INTELLIGENCE SUMMARY.
(Erase heading not required.)

May 1917

Instructions regarding War Diaries and Intelligence Summaries are contained in F. S. Regs., Part II. and the Staff Manual respectively. Title pages will be prepared in manuscript.

Place	Date	Hour	Summary of Events and Information	Remarks and references to Appendices
In the Field	26 to 31		This unit provided working parties and transport at SWINDON Pulhead and LINDENHOEK (R.F.A.) for the purpose taking up ammunition to Battery positions of 32nd Divisional Artillery, and in three 5 days 54,000 rounds of ammunition were taken up to gun positions. Convoys & parks were heavily shelled, but the only casualty was 1 mule killed, and 9 wounded. Ammunition Received during work including amount mentioned in last para above. Approx. 49,000 rds. 18 pr. ammn. 15,000 " 4.5 " Issued including above mentioned amount and ammunition returned to Railhead. Approx. 42,000 rounds 18 pr. ammn. 19,000 " 4.5 "	/s- /s- /s
	29		Mentions in Despatches. Capt. J.E.F. HARLEY of this unit received mention in C. in C.'s despatch of 29th May 1917. Revd R.E. GRICE-HUTCHINSON, attached to this unit as Chaplain to 32nd Divl. Arty received mention in C. in C's despatch of 29th May 1917.	/s

T. Walker Lieut. Col.
Commdg. 32nd. Div. Ammn. Coln, R.F.A.

Vol 18

Confidential.

32nd Divisional
Ammunition Column,
R.F.A.

"War Diary."

1 - 30 June 1917.

30 June 1917.

Army Form C. 2118.

WAR DIARY
INTELLIGENCE SUMMARY.
(Erase heading not required.)

JUNE 1917

Place	Date	Hour	Summary of Events and Information	Remarks and references to Appendices
In the Field.	JUNE 4th		**OFFICERS.** 2/Lieut. H.D. BOYD rejoined the unit from C.C.S.	
-do-	JUNE 5th		**CASUALTIES.** 1. other rank wounded - remained at duty.	
-do-	JUNE 6th		1. other rank wounded - admitted to hospital.	
-do-	JUNE 6th		**DETACHMENTS.** The S.A.A. Section of this unit comprising 5 Officers and 210 other ranks with necessary animals and vehicles under the command of Major J.F.K. LOCKHART, was detailed from this unit and proceeded to NEUF BERQUIN (Ref. I.5. HAZEBROUCK Sheet 5a) in readiness for ammunition supply to 32nd Division Infantry. This detachment rejoined the unit on the 11th inst.	
-do-	JUNE 11th		**MOVE.** The unit moved from BAILLEUL to NONE BOSCHE Farm (Ref. Q.4.c Sheet 27)	
-do-	JUNE 14th		The unit moved from NONE BOSCHE Farm to WORMHOUDT (Ref. C.17.a Sheet 27)	
-do-	JUNE 16th		The unit moved from WORMHOUDT to PONT DE PETITE SYNTHE (Ref. H.25.a. Sheet 19)	
-do-	JUNE 18th		The unit moved from PONT DE PETITE SYNTHE to MALO TERMINUS (Ref. C.14.d. Sheet 19)	
-do-	JUNE 22nd		"B" Echelon of this unit moved from MALO TERMINUS to BRIQUETERIE VAN HOVE (Ref. X.27.a. Sheet 11)	
-do-	JUNE 23rd		The remainder of the unit moved from MALO TERMINUS to 32nd Division Area, Headquarters being established at FERME DEBANTT. (Ref. X.21.a. Sheet 11)	
-do-	JUNE 24th		**CASUALTY** No 14818, Driver H. BROUGHTON was accidentally drowned whilst bathing in the FURNES - NIEUPORT Canal	
-do-	JUNE 25th		**DECORATION.** Notification was received that 2/Lieut. P.R. HAMILTON of No 1 Section of this unit had been awarded the Military Cross for gallantry performed whilst engaged on an ammunition dump run by this unit in connection with the MESSINES - WYTSCHAETE Ridge battle on the 8th inst, during the time this unit was attached to the 36th Divisional Artillery	

22ND DIVISIONAL AMMUNITION COLUMN R.F.A.

Army Form C. 2118.

WAR DIARY
or
INTELLIGENCE SUMMARY.
(Erase heading not required.)

SHEET 2.   JUNE 1917.

Instructions regarding War Diaries and Intelligence Summaries are contained in F. S. Regs., Part II. and the Staff Manual respectively. Title pages will be prepared in manuscript.

Place	Date	Hour	Summary of Events and Information	Remarks and references to Appendices
In the Field.	JUNE 26th		CASUALTY. 1. other rank wounded – remained at duty.	/5
			AMMUNITION. Gun Ammunition received during the month A 6936 AX 4464 BX 2872	/5
			Gun Ammunition delivered during the month. 5824 4464 2872	/5
			REINFORCEMENTS. 157 other ranks, reinforcements joined this unit from Base during the month and were distributed to units of the 32nd Divisional Artillery.	/5

[signed] Lieut Col^l
Commdg. 32nd. Div. Ammn. Col., R.F.A.

<u>Confidential</u>

<u>War Diary</u>
— of —
<u>32nd Divisional Ammunition Column,</u>
<u>— R.F.A. —</u>

<u>From, 1st July 1917</u>
<u>To, 31st July 1917</u>

WAR DIARY
or
INTELLIGENCE SUMMARY

Army Form C. 2118.

JULY 1917

Place	Date	Hour	Summary of Events and Information	Remarks and references to Appendices
In the Field.	1917 JULY 10th		CASUALTIES. During the attack on the YSER CANAL, this unit had 1 other rank killed and 13, other ranks wounded by hostile shell fire, on this date. 4 animals were also killed and 23 wounded by hostile shell fire on this date.	A/S.
-do-	JULY 11th		DECORATIONS. Notification was received on this date that No. 13950, Gunner BACON, E, attached to this unit, had been awarded the Military Medal, for conspicuous work in the MESSINES battle.	A/S.
-do-	JULY 15th		AMMUNITION. A gun ammunition dump was formed on this date at X.8.b. (Ref. Sheet 11) : This was called the "Hull Dump". It was taken over by the 49th Division on 23/7/17.	A/S.
-do-	JULY 27th		OFFICERS. Notification was received on this date that 2/Lieut. R.H. THOMPSON (T.F.) had been promoted Lieutenant, with precedence, as and from June 1st 1916.	A/S.
-do-	JULY 31st		DECORATIONS. Notification was received on this date that No 14939, Sergt CLINTON H. and No. 13921, Corporal HORNBY H. had been awarded the Military Medal, for conspicuous work in the MESSINES battle.	A/S.
-do-	JULY 30th		REINFORCEMENTS. 75 other ranks, reinforcements arrived from Base on this date, and were distributed to units of the 32nd Divisional Artillery.	A/S.

Army Form C. 2118.

WAR DIARY
or
INTELLIGENCE SUMMARY.

(Erase heading not required.)

Place	Date	Hour	Summary of Events and Information	Remarks and references to Appendices
IN the Field.			AMMUNITION. During the month, the following gun ammunition has been delivered and/or issued :- A. 116084 rds. 4.5" SMOKE, and } AX. 55326 " GAS Ammunition.} 2464. rds. BX. 48992 " The Brigades supplied were:- 14th Army Bde, R.H.A. 72nd Army Bde, R.F.A. 175th Army Bde, R.F.A. 32nd Divisional Artillery. 66th -do- 49th -do- 3rd Aust. Army F.A. Bde. 6th -do- 12th -do- As the situations of this unit's main dump and many of the Batteries were on or near the banks of the FURNES-NIEUPORT Canal, it was considered that transportation of ammunition by barge was possible. Accordingly several barges were obtained from Transportation Dept. and by this mode, a considerable amount of ammunition was delivered to batteries in a very short time. Had barges been available earlier, it would have been possible to send up by this means a much larger amount of ammunition in the time. As it was, however, an appreciable saving of horseflesh, diminution of traffic congestion and possible saving of roads, were effected. the following mentioned figures, the above mentioned figures, the following ammunition was delivered by barge. A. 29776 AX. 13444 BX. 15974. In addition the barges were used for the carriage of Decauville rails, to proximity of Battery positions.	

Lieut. Col.
Comdg. 32nd Div. Ammn. Col., R.F.A.

Confidential

War Diary
— of —
32nd Divisional Ammunition Column R.F.A.

1w. period

1st to 31st August 1917.

Army Form C. 2118.

WAR DIARY
or
INTELLIGENCE SUMMARY.
(Erase heading not required.)

AUGUST 1917.

92ND DIVISIONAL AMMUNITION COLUMN R.F.A.

Place	Date	Hour	Summary of Events and Information	Remarks and references to Appendices
In the Field.	AUGUST 3rd		CASUALTIES. 2 other ranks wounded by hostile shell fire.	/ho
-do-	7th		1 other rank wounded by hostile shell fire.	/ho
-do-	10th		1 other rank accidentally drowned in the FURNES-NIEUPORT CANAL, whilst one of a party on an ammunition barge. 2/Lieut. F.R. HAMILTON, M.C. in charge of this units forward dump at the PONT DU PELICAN, (Reference S. 4. a. Sheet 12), was seriously wounded by hostile shell fire. 8 other ranks were wounded by hostile shell fire, 1 of whom subsequently died of wounds.	/ho
-do-	10th		ATTACHMENTS. 1 Officer and 36 other ranks were attached to this unit from 158th Army Bde, R.F.A. to assist in work on this unit's main ammunition dump.	/ho
-do-	12th		CASUALTIES. 4 other ranks were wounded by hostile shell fire.	/ho
-do-	14th		1 other rank was wounded by hostile shell fire.	/ho
-do-	15th		ACT OF COURAGE. No. 15647, Driver J.T. TATTERSFIELD of this unit was mentioned in Fourth Army Routine Orders, for an act of courage, performed in connection with the stopping of runaway horses.	/ho
			AMMUNITION SUPPLY. Throughout the month, this unit continued the supply of ammunition to 6 groups of Field Artillery, comprising 27 batteries, mainly by barge transport on the FURNES-NIEUPORT CANAL. At the end of this month (August 1917), this unit had on charge 13 barges and one motor launch for the delivery of ammunition. During the month the following ammunition transactions have taken place. A. A.X. B.X. Smoke and Gas Ammtn. RECEIVED. 71774 47052 29258 6102 ISSUED. 50171 35599 29522 2478	/ho
			REINFORCEMENTS. 97 reinforcements have been received during the month from Base and distributed to units of 32nd Divisional Artillery.	/ho

Lieut. Col.
Commdg. 32nd. Div. Ammn. Col., R.F.A.

Headquarters,

32nd Divisional Artillery.

Reference the attached, nothing of importance, worthy of record, occurred in connection with this unit between the 15th and 31st August 1917, please.

J. Johnson Capt. & Adjutant,
For Officer Commanding,
32nd Div. Ammtn. Col. R.F.A.

4th August 1917.

HQ 32nd Division.

Forwarded.

Maurice
Lieut Colonel RFA
CRA 32nd Division

Vol 21

Confidential

War Diary
of
32nd Divisional Ammunition Column R.F.A.

Period:- 1st to 30th September 1917.

Army Form C. 2118

WAR DIARY
or
INTELLIGENCE SUMMARY
(Erase heading not required.)

Instructions regarding War Diaries and Intelligence Summaries are contained in F. S. Regs., Part II. and the Staff Manual respectively. Title Pages will be prepared in manuscript.

SEPTEMBER, 1917.

Place	Date	Hour	Summary of Events and Information	Remarks and references to Appendices
In the Field.	1st		OFFICERS. 2/Lieut. P.R. HAMILTON, M.C., struck off the strength with effect from 10/8/17 vowed.	/xx
-do-	2nd		2/Lieut. F.J. SCOTT, No 1 Section, posted to V.52.T.M.Battery.	/xx
-do-	7		CASUALTIES. 1 o.r. wounded by hostile shell fire: Admitted hospital.	/xx
"	"		DUMPS. This Unit took over "HULL DUMP" of ammunition at X.8.b.3.6.(Sheet 11) from 49th Divisional Artillery and continued its management up to the present time.	/15
"	10th		CASUALTIES. 1 o.r. wounded by hostile artillery fire: admitted hospital.	/xx
"	"		OFFICERS. 2/Lieut. F.W. GILES rejoined this Unit after attachment to IV Corps Ammunition Park	/xx
"	"		CASUALTIES. 1 o.r. wounded by hostile shell fire; admitted hospital.	/xx
"	16th		HOSTILE SHELLING. This Unit's "CANAL DUMP" at X.27.a.(Sheet 11) was shelled by the enemy at intervals during the night with about 40 H.E. No casualties.	/xx
"	17th		BARGE TRANSPORT. I.W.T. Barge No A.59 whilst engaged carrying ammunition on the Canal near NIEUPORT was sunk at about 12 midnight, through the sudden opening of a sluice running into the Canal. 1 o.r. was drowned.	/xx
"	19th		OFFICERS. Lt. A.B. Heinemann formerly of this Unit, rejoined from Base.	/xx
"	27th		REWARDS. No L/15696 Dvr. W. BUCKBERRY Of No 2 Section of this Unit, was awarded the Military Medal by G.O.C. XVth Corps for devotion to duty and commendable conduct whilst driver of a runaway team with ammunition wagon near the front system of trenches under heavy shell fire.	/xx
"	"		REINFORCEMENTS. 58 Reinforcements joined this Unit from Base during the month, and were distributed to Units of 32nd Divisional Artillery.	/xx

[signature] Lieut. Col.
Commdg. 32nd. Div. Ammn. Col., R.F.A.

Army Form C. 2118

WAR DIARY
or
INTELLIGENCE SUMMARY

SEPTEMBER 1917. (Page 2).

(Erase heading not required.)

Instructions regarding War Diaries and Intelligence Summaries are contained in F. S. Regs., Part II. and the Staff Manual respectively. Title Pages will be prepared in manuscript.

Place	Date	Hour	Summary of Events and Information	Remarks and references to Appendices
			AMMUNITION. Throughout the month, this Unit continued the supply of ammunition to the Right Divisional Artillery of XVth Corps, comprising six Brigades of Field artillery. Supply was mainly from the "CANAL DUMP" by barge transport to the vicinity of NIEUPORT sector. In addition a quantity of gun ammunition was brought back from vacated gun positions and cleaned, sorted and re-boxed for further issue. This work is still continuing. The barge transport was also utilized for various other work, i.e., transport of Infantry parties to the forward area; carriage of stores, material etc. Ammunition transactions during the month are as follows:-	/3
			A. AX. BX. GAS etc. Receipts. 10,789 6575 8974 684 } being amount of ammunition brought back from vacated positions Issues. 25,638 16277 8950 1374 } Includes "Hull Dump" transactions and ammunition returned to Railhead.	/3
			LOCATION OF UNIT. Remained the same during the month, viz: Headquarters at X.21.c.8.7 (sheet 11).	/3

Walker Lieut. Col.
Commdg. 32nd. Div. Ammn. Col., R.F.A.

Confidential

War Diary
of
32nd Divisional Ammunition Column,
R.F.A

From 1st October 1917.
To 31st October 1917.

Army Form C. 2118

WAR DIARY
or
INTELLIGENCE SUMMARY
(Erase heading not required.)

OCTOBER 1917.

Instructions regarding War Diaries and Intelligence Summaries are contained in F.S. Regs., Part II. and the Staff Manual respectively. Title Pages will be prepared in manuscript.

Place	Date	Hour	Summary of Events and Information	Remarks and references to Appendices
In the Field.	OCTOBER 8th		CASUALTIES. 1 other rank wounded by hostile shell fire.	
—do—	9th		1 other rank killed by hostile shell fire.	
—do—	13th		MOVE. The unit moved from the NIEUPORT area to GHYVELDE (Ref.D.22.a. Sheet 19)., after handing over CANAL DUMP, HULL DUMP etc. to the 42nd Div. Amm. Col.	
—do—	15th		The unit continued the move to WORMHOUDT (Ref. C. 17.a. Sheet 27)	
—do—	17th		The unit continued the move to the vicinity of POPERINGHE (Ref.F.28.b. Sheet 27)	
—do—	18th		The unit moved to B.26.a.4.1. (Ref. Sheet 28) and took over from the 51st D.A.C.	
—do—	18th		SUPPLY OF AMMUNITION. The unit commenced the supply of ammunition to 34th, 82nd, 161st and 282nd Brigades, R.F.A. under the direction of 18th Divisional Artillery. All ammunition was carried to the Battery positions by pack transport, owing to the condition of the roads East of YPRES.	
—do—	22nd		CASUALTIES. 3 other ranks wounded by hostile shell fire.	
—do—	28th		2 other ranks wounded by hostile shell fire.	
—do—	29th		1 other rank killed by hostile shell fire.	
—do—	29th		OFFICERS. Major J.F.K. LOCKHART (attached to this unit) posted to the 161st Brigade, R.F.A.	
—do—	30th		CASUALTIES. 2 other ranks wounded by hostile shell fire.	

AMMUNITION TRANSACTIONS. during the month are as follows:-

	A	AX	BX	GAS. etc.
RECEIVED.	18026	14333	6168	2872
	3404	2032	1232	650
ISSUED.	17367	14855	6176	2872 ---by pack transport:
	5435	4080	5440	10898 ---handed over on leaving Fourth Army Area.

AMMUNITION SALVED IN FIFTH ARMY AREA. 2644   1554   753   32

REINFORCEMENTS. 50pr—2 rds. T.M. 9.45—150 rds. Much of this was unserviceable joined the unit from the Base during the month and were distributed to units of 32nd Divisional Artillery.

LOCATION OF UNIT AT END OF THE MONTH. B.26.a.4.1. (Sheet 28)

Lieut. Col.
Commdg. 32nd. Div. Ammn. Col. R.F.A.

Vol 23

Confidential

War Diary
— of —
32nd Divisional Ammunition Column R.F.A.

From 1st to 30th November 1917.

Army Form C. 2118.

WAR DIARY
or
INTELLIGENCE-SUMMARY.
(Erase heading not required.)

NOVEMBER 1917.

Instructions regarding War Diaries and Intelligence Summaries are contained in F.S. Regs., Part II. and the Staff Manual respectively. Title pages will be prepared in manuscript.

Place	Date	Hour	Summary of Events and Information	Remarks and references to Appendices
In the Field.	4/11/17		CASUALTIES. 1 other rank wounded by enemy shell fire.	I.S.I.
-do-	8/11/17		1 other rank wounded by enemy shell fire.	I.S.I.
-do-	9/11/17		3 other ranks wounded by hostile shell fire (2 of these subsequently died of wounds)	I.S.I. I.S.I.
-do-	14/11/17		1 other rank wounded by enemy shell fire.	I.S.I.
-do-	22/11/17.		DUMPS, etc. This unit detached 1 Officer and 34 other ranks, together with transport and animals to work 32nd Division Infantry ammunition dump, near YPRES.	I.S.I.
-do-	23/11/17.		CASUALTIES. 1 other rank wounded by enemy shell fire.	I.S.I. I.S.I.
-do-	24/11/17		On this date this unit came under the administration of 32nd Divisional Artillery.	I.S.I.
-do-	24/11/17		DUMPS, etc. This unit took over from 1st Division, the management of BUFF ROAD gun ammunition dump, near YPRES.	I.S.I. I.S.I.
-do-	29/11/17.		CASUALTIES. 3 other ranks wounded by hostile shelling of "B" Echelon lines of the unit.	
-do-	30/11/17		2 other ranks killed and 3 other ranks wounded whilst on ammunition convoy.	
			AMMUNITION TRANSACTIONS. Received during the month. 18 pr. 4.5" Smoke,Gas,etc. 60250 21574 1296 } Includes Issued during the month. 52207 19411 260 } transactions at ZOUAVE DUMP. The following ammunition has been salved and disposed of during the month. 18 pr. 4480, 4.5". 1679. Miscellaneous, i.e. 71 8" T.M. 60 pr.,etc.}	I.S.I.
			In addition a large number of cartridge cases, etc have been salved and returned to Railheads.	I.S.I.
			REINFORCEMENTS. 289 reinforcements have joined from Base during the month and have been distributed to units of 32nd Divisional Artillery.	I.S.I.
			LOCATION OF UNIT at end of the month,(H.Q.) E.26.a.4.1, Sheet 28.	I.S.I.

Commdg. 32nd. Div. Ammn. Col., R.F.A.
Lieut. Col.

Confidential

War Diary
of
32nd Divisional Ammunition Column R.F.A.

From 1st to 31st December 1917.

Army Form C. 2118

WAR DIARY
or
INTELLIGENCE SUMMARY

DECEMBER 1917.

(Erase heading not required.)

Instructions regarding War Diaries and Intelligence Summaries are contained in F. S. Regs., Part II. and the Staff Manual respectively. Title Pages will be prepared in manuscript.

32ND DIVISIONAL AMMUNITION COLUMN R.F.A.

Place	Date	Hour	Summary of Events and Information	Remarks and references to Appendices
In the Field.	9/12/17		CASUALTIES. 1 other rank slightly wounded by hostile fire.	1/65
-do-	9/12/17		3 other ranks slightly wounded by enemy aircraft bomb which was dropped in camp.	1/65
-do-	12/12/17		OFFICERS. Major J.F.K. LOCKHART, F.F.A. joined this unit for attachment from A/161 Battery F.F.A.	1/65
-do-			HONOURS DESPATCH. The following of this unit were mentioned in the Commander-in-Chief's Honour's Despatch of November 7th 1917. (London Gazette 11/12/17) Lieut.Col. J. WALKER, D.S.O. Lieut. B. MONK. L/15958, F.S.M. BRYDEN, H.	1/65
-do-	15/12/17		GUN POOL. On the 14th December this unit took over the Gun Pool of the 52nd Divisional Artillery Group from the 1st Divisional Artillery. To the end of the month the following Guns and Howitzers have passed through the Gun Pool whilst under the management of this unit. 4 18pr guns - 4 4.5" Hows.	1/65
-do-	15/12/17		CASUALTIES. 1 other rank slightly wounded by hostile fire.	1/65
-do-	20/12/17		REORGANIZATION. This unit on 20/12/17 was reorganized on War Establishment No. 642. "B" Echelon of this unit became the S.A.A. Section, and the remaining two Sections which previously formed "A" Echelon, became No's 1 and 2 Sections respectively. The surplus personnel and animals accruing on this reorganization were distributed mainly to Units of the 32nd Divisional Artillery. No further incidents worthy of record occurred after this date.	1/65

J. Walker Lieut. Col.
Commdg. 32nd. Div. Ammn. Col., R.F.A.

Army Form C. 2118

WAR DIARY
or
INTELLIGENCE SUMMARY   DECEMBER 1917.
(Erase heading not required.)

Instructions regarding War Diaries and Intelligence Summaries are contained in F.S. Regs., Part II. and the Staff Manual respectively. Title Pages will be prepared in manuscript.

Place	Date	Hour	Summary of Events and Information	Remarks and references to Appendices

In the Field.			SALVAGE. During the month this unit gave considerable attention to the salvage work on the area forward of YPRES and the following figures shew ammunition and components salved during the month.
			      18 pr. ammtn. 7888 rounds.
			      4.5. ammtn. 3941 "
			      Cartridge cases 18 pr 98094
			           -do- 4.5. 6974
			 In addition various other salvage work on derelict guns, etc was performed.
			
			 AMMUNITION TRANSACTIONS. during the month were as follows.
			    RECEIPTS.
			      18 pr ammtn. 76164 rounds
			      4.5. ammtn. 51434 "
			      Smoke etc ammtn. 1702 "
			    ISSUES.
			      18 pr ammtn. 37653 rounds.
			      4.5 ammtn. 11326 "
			      Smoke etc ammtn. 996 "
			
			 REINFORCEMENTS. 92 other ranks reinforcements joined this unit from Base during the month and were distributed to units of 32nd Divisional Artillery.
			
			 LOCATIONS of the unit at the end of the month, B.26.a.4.1. Sheet 28, (same as previous month)
				/ks
				
				 /k
				
				 /ks
				
				 /ks /ks

Includes transactions at BUFFS ROAD Ammunition Dump.

J. Walker Lieut. Col.
Commdg. 32nd. Div. Ammn. Col, R.F.A.

Confidential

Vol 25

— War Diary —
of
32ⁿᵈ Divisional Ammunition Column
R.F.A.

1ˢᵗ to 31ˢᵗ January 1918.

Army Form C. 2118

WAR DIARY
or
INTELLIGENCE SUMMARY
JANUARY, 1918.

(Erase heading not required.)

Instructions regarding War Diaries and Intelligence Summaries are contained in F. S. Regs., Part II. and the Staff Manual respectively. Title Pages will be prepared in manuscript.

[Stamp: 32ND DIVISIONAL AMMUNITION COLUMN R.F.A.]

Place	Date	Hour	Summary of Events and Information	Remarks and references to Appendices
In the Field.	6/1/18		CASUALTIES. 2 other ranks wounded by hostile shelling of Lines. (Both died of wounds)	
-do-	8/1/18.		OFFICERS. 2/Lieut.C.F.REED.R.F.A.(T) joined this Unit from Base.	
-do-	22/1/18.		-do- Major.J.F.K.LOCKHART.R.F.A. was posted from this Unit to 52nd Div.Arty.	
			GENERAL REMARKS. Nothing further of note happened in connection with this Unit during the month.	
			AMMUNITION TRANSACTIONS were practically Nil from 8th January to end of the month, the 32nd Div.Arty was withdrawn to Wagon Lines for rest and during this time this Unit was occupied in Training, Gun Drill, Improvement of Stables etc.,	
			REINFORCEMENTS. 104 Reinforcements arrived from Base and were posted to Units of 32nd Div.Arty.	
			LOCATION of the Unit at the end of the month, B.25.a.4.1.(Sheet 28 same as previous month)	
-do-	28/1/18.		DUMPS. This Unit took over from the 1st Division & 18th Division the two S.A.A.Dumps at(Nr GEDDES DUMP) T.27.d.4.7.(Sheet 20.S.W.)and GOUVY FARM B.11.a.6.5.upon the 32nd Division taking over a front previously held by two Divisions.	
-do-	31/1/18.		This Unit took over the A.R.P at WULVERTON B.6.d.2.6. (Sheet 28) from the 18th Division.	

Johnson Capt.
& Adjutant,
For Officer Commanding,
32nd Div. Ammtn. Col. R.F.A.

Confidential

War Diary
— of —

32nd Divisional Ammunition Column R.F.A.

Period :- 1st to 28th February 1918.

Army Form C. 2118.

WAR DIARY
or
INTELLIGENCE SUMMARY

(Erase heading not required.)

FEBRUARY 1918.

Instructions regarding War Diaries and Intelligence Summaries are contained in F.S. Regs., Part II. and the Staff Manual respectively. Title Pages will be prepared in manuscript.

(stamp: 32nd DIVISIONAL AMMUNITION COLUMN No. ___ R.F.A.)

Place	Date	Hour	Summary of Events and Information	Remarks and references to Appendices
In the Field.	1918. Feb.11th		**DUMPS.** WOLVERTON DUMP was handed over the 35th Division on this date. GEDDES DUMP situate T.27.c.c. (Sheet 28) was taken over on this date, and came under the direction of this unit.	
	Feb.16th		**COURSE.** A party of 2 Officers and 4 N.C.O's proceeded to Advanced Indian Base Depot at ROUEN to undergo a course in "Handling of Indians" in preparation for Indian personnel expected to join this unit in March 1918.	

	Feb.17th		**SALVAGE.** Salvage operations of the Divisional area were undertaken by a party from this unit under the charge of an Officer, and to the end of the month, the following ammunition was salved.
			    18pr. 3728 Rounds.
			    4.5" 3514 "
			  Miscellaneous. 1055 " including French and German ammunition, etc.
			A large number of empty cartridge cases and other material was also salved.
			AMMUNITION. Transactions during the month have been small and are as follows:—
			  Receipts. 18pr 1448
			             4.5" 4924
			  Issues. 18pr 5371
			             4.5" 1700
			          Smoke,etc 231
			REINFORCEMENTS. 90 reinforcements arrived during the month and were distributed to units of 32nd Divisional Artillery.
			Nothing of importance affecting this unit, occurred during the month.
			LOCATION OF UNIT. At end of the month. B.26.a.4.1. (Sheet 28), same as preceding month.	

_____
Lieut. Col.
Commdg. 32nd. Div. Ammn. Col, R.F.A.

32nd Divisional Artillery.

32nd DIVISIONAL AMMUNITION COLUMN R.F.A.

MARCH 1 9 1 8

Vol 27

Confidential

War Diary
of
32nd Divisional Ammunition Column R.F.A.

Period:- 1st to 31st March 1918.

WAR DIARY
or
INTELLIGENCE SUMMARY   MARCH 1918

Army Form C. 2118

Place	Date	Hour	Summary of Events and Information	Remarks and references to Appendices
In Field	1918 March 5th	Officers	Lt H.S.A WHITE RFA (S.R.) taken on strength of this Unit and remained attached to II Corps Counter-Battery Office.	/to
	6th	Move	This Units HQ and No. 1 Section moved to TROIS TOURS Chateauarea, BRIELEN.	/to
	10th	Drafts	This Unit took over the management of WOLVERTON Dump from 35th Division.	/to
	13th	Indian Personnel	Lt G.E. Fotherby, Lt M.D Boyd and 4 NCO's of this Unit has returned from Course of "Handling of Indians" notification having been received that Indian personnel was not yet available for this Unit.	/to
	26th	Officers	Lt Col F.B Aykroo, DSO, RFA. was attached to this Unit until posted to command of 223" Brigade RFA on 29.3.18.	/to
	26th	Moves.	A portion of SAA Section of this Unit today entrained with 97th Infantry Brigade for Third Army area.	/to
	29th	"	Remainder of SAA Section today entrained for Third Army Area and re-established at GAUDIEMPRÉ.	/to
	31st	"	This Unit (less SAA Section) entrained for Third Army Area and re-established itself on this day at HAUTEVILLE.	/to
	30th	Dumps	GEDDES Dump and WOLVERTON Dump, in II Corps Area, were this day handed over to 1st Divisional Artillery.	/to

Ammunition Transactions during the month are as follows:-

Receipts   18pr   446695 rds.
            15 hr   1200 "
            4.5   3048   "

Cont. page 2.

WAR DIARY
INTELLIGENCE SUMMARY — MARCH 1918 (Page 2)

(Erase heading not required.)

Place	Date	Hour	Summary of Events and Information	Remarks and references to Appendices
			Ammunition Transactions (continued)	
			Issues 18 p^r 30491 rds 15 p^r 12100 " 4·5" 5566 " G.o.ch. 159 " } exclusive of handing-over transactions.	/w /w
			Salvage The following salvage has been collected by this Unit during the month:—	
			18 p^r 4·5" Rds Cases Rds Cases Charges Miscellaneous Ammn. 11790 51842 1906 9630 6450 109 rds.	
			Also:— 6 G.S. wagon loads barbed wire sorted into S&A. 2 35 fuzes No 201 1 Wagon body (60 pdr). 12 Wheels No^s 4·5 1 Limber RE Store wagon 3 firet Bearings, G.S. wagon 3 Linchpins 18 p^r. 1 4·5" Howitzer, Armoured.	Running out Springs Periscopt Air Respirator fronts 4 Wheels 10 D.0 1 heavy Gun wheel. 3 Fore Carriage G.S. wagon 1 axle 1 Hand Cart. 2 Ammunition Wagon bodies 18 p^r. Various parts of G.S. wagons.	/w
			Reinforcements 52 Reinforcements joined from Base and were distributed to Units of 32nd Divisional Artillery.	/w
			Location of Unit's HQ at end of month, The Chateau HAUTEVILLE (Refer Sheet 51c J 35 c. Central)	/w

J. Walker Lieut. Col.
Commdg. 32nd. Div. Ammn. Col., R.F.A.

VI.Corps.
Third Army.

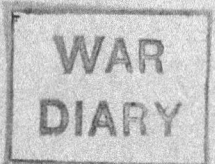

32nd DIVISIONAL AMMUNITION COLUMN, R.F.A.

A P R I L

1 9 1 8

Vol 28

Confidential

War Diary

— of —

32nd Divisional Ammunition Column R.F.A.

Period. 1st to 30th April 1918.

Army Form C. 2118

WAR DIARY
or
INTELLIGENCE SUMMARY — APRIL 1918.
(Erase heading not required.)

Place	Date	Hour	Summary of Events and Information	Remarks and references to Appendices
Field	3-4-1918 4-4-18		**Moves.** This Unit (less S.A.A. Section) moved from HAUTEVILLE to LA BAZEQUE (Ref.51c./V.21.). Unit (less S.A.A. Section) moved to GAUDIEMPRE (Ref.51c./V.25.d) and joined S.A.A. Section of this Unit.	J.W.H.L.
	6th		**Dumps.** This Unit took over POMMIER Ammunition Refilling Point from 31st Divisional Artillery and recommenced ammunition supply to 32nd Divisional Artillery.	J.W.H.L.
	12th 12th		**Casualties.** 1 o.r. wounded (A.A. rifle)—remained at duty. Officers. 2/Lieut. E.H. WEIHE taken on strength from 161st Brigade R.F.A. and posted to 32nd Division Trench Mortar Batteries on 27th April 1918.	J.W.H.L. J.W.H.L.
	25th		**Moves.** S.A.A. Section of this Unit moved out with 32nd Division Infantry and re-established at SOMBRIN (Ref.51c./O.23).	J.W.H.L.
	28th		The remainder of this Unit moved to GOUY-en-ARTOIS (Ref.51c./F.18.a) on 32nd Divisional Artillery becoming attached to 40th Divisional Artillery.	J.W.H.L.
	29th		**Dumps.** POMMIER A.R.P. was handed over to Guards Divisional Artillery.	J.W.H.L.
			Ammunition Transactions during the month are as follows:-	
			Receipts:- 18pr. 4.5" Gas etc.	
			95,598 17,442 6,290 } Includes dump transactions.	J.W.H.L.
			Issues:- 68,311 10,832 5,786	
			" S.A.A. .303	
			Salvage. The following have been salved by the Unit during the month:-	
			Cartridge cases 18pr. 19,789	
			" 4.5" 3,600	
			S.A.A. .303 42,000	
			Also numerous loads of F.E. material, clothing etc.	
			Reinforcements. 105 Reinforcements have joined from Base during the month and have been posted to Units of 32nd Divisional Artillery.	J.W.H.L.
			Location of Units H.Q. at end of month:- GOUY-en-ARTOIS:	J.W.H.L.

J. _____
Lieut. Col.
Commdg. 32nd. Div. Ammn. Col., R.F.A.

Vol 29

Confidential

War Diary

of

32nd Divisional Ammunition Column R.F.A.

1st to 31st May 1918.

WAR DIARY or INTELLIGENCE SUMMARY

Army Form C. 2118

MAY 1918.

(Erase heading not required.)

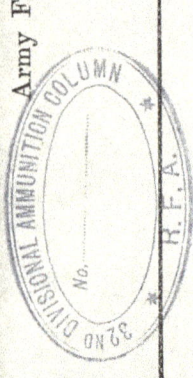

32ND DIVISIONAL AMMUNITION COLUMN R.F.A.

Place	Date	Hour	Summary of Events and Information	Remarks and references to Appendices
In the Field	1918 May 5		**Dumps of ammunition.** A new forward dump of gun ammunition, called "BELLA" Dump was commenced by this Unit on this date.	1.w.
	" 12		**Moves.** S.A.A. Section of this Unit moved from SOMERIN (Ref.Sheet 51c/P.18.d). No 2 Section of this Unit moved from GOUY-en-ARTOIS to lines at W.5.c. sheet 51c.	1.w.
	" 14		**Attachment.** No 1 Section 39th Divisional Ammunition Column R.F.A. became attached to this Unit on this date, for purposes of ammunition supply etc. Reinforcements. 12 gunners were supplied by this Unit to batteries of 32nd Divisional Artillery to replace casualties.	1.w.
	" 15		**Ammunition Supply Practice** under mobile warfare conditions was practised under instructions from VI Corps.	1.w.
	" 16		**Ammunition Dumps.** On 32nd Divisional Artillery H.Q. taking over command of Left Divisional Artillery of VI Corps from X 40th Divisional Artillery, BLAIREVILLE Artillery Ammunition Dump came under this Unit's direction. Casualties. 1 o.r. wounded (A.A. fire).	1.w. 1.w.
	" 20		**Moves.** S.A.A. Section of this Unit moved from GOUY-en-ARTOIS to lines at W.9.c., sheet 51c. Officers. Lieut. P.R. Hamilton M.C. R.F.A. formerly of this Unit, taken on the strength from 49th Divisional Artillery. Lieut. A.B. Heinemann R.F.A.(T) of this Unit posted to 168th Brigade R.F.A. as Adviser in artillery horse lines.	1.w.
	" 21		**Working party.** A party of 1 Officer and 30 o.r. of this Unit (along with personnel from other units of 32nd Divisional Artillery) commenced special work in cable-burying in the forward area.	1.w.
	" 25		**Casualties.** 1 o.r. wounded by enemy shell fire.	1.w.
	" 26			

WAR DIARY
— of —
INTELLIGENCE SUMMARY   MAY 1918   (page 1).
(Erase heading not required.)

Army Form C. 2118

Instructions regarding War Diaries and Intelligence Summaries are contained in F.S. Regs., Part II. and the Staff Manual respectively. Title Pages will be prepared in manuscript.

Place	Date	Hour	Summary of Events and Information	Remarks and references to Appendices
In the Field	1918 May 30		Casualties. 1 O.R. slightly wounded; remained at duty.	1.05.
	31		—do— 3 o.r. wounded by enemy M.G. fire.	1.00.
			Ammunition transactions during the month were as follows:—	
			18pr. 4.5" Gas, etc.	
			Receipts 74,555 27,908 5,654 } Includes transactions at	
			Issues. 64,324 18,196 5,218 } ammunition dumps.	
			Salvage. The following salvage has been collected by this Unit during the month:—	
			Cartridge cases 18pr. 3,782	
			Charge Cases 4.5" 7,800	
			Reinforcements. 96 Reinforcements have joined this Unit during the month from Base, and have been distributed to Units of 32nd Divisional Artillery.	
			Location of Headquarters of the Unit at the end of the month:— GOUY-en-ARTOIS.	

J. Waller   Lieut. Col.
Commdg. 32nd. Div. Ammn. Col., R.F.A.

Confidential.

Vol 30

War Diary

of

32nd Divisional Ammunition Column,
R.F.A.

Period. 1st June 1918.
to
30th June 1918.

Army Form C. 2118

WAR DIARY
or
INTELLIGENCE SUMMARY

(Erase heading not required.)

Instructions regarding War Diaries and Intelligence Summaries are contained in F. S. Regs., Part II. and the Staff Manual respectively. Title Pages will be prepared in manuscript.

JUNE 1918.

Place	Date	Hour	Summary of Events and Information	Remarks and references to Appendices
In the Field.	2/6/18		CASUALTIES. 1 other rank wounded on this date.	
	7/6/18		OFFICERS. Lieut. P.F. HAMILTON, M.C. posted to 161st Brigade, R.F.A.	
	9/6/18		Lieut. H.S.A. WHITE (S.R.) posted to 6th Divisional Artillery.	
	14/6/18		HONOURS AND AWARDS. The Military Medal was awarded to:- No. L/14022, Sergt. Rainton, C. No. L/14032, Driver W.F. Stathers, of this unit, in connection with a gas projector scheme.	
	18/6/18		ATTACHMENTS. No. 1 Section, 39th D.A.C. rejoined their unit on this date.	
	20/6/18		ATTACHMENTS. 72nd Army Brigade Amm.Col. F.F.A. and 155th Army Brigade Amm. Col. F.F.A. came under the direction of this unit on this date.	
	20/6/18		REORGANIZATION of the Column took place in accordance with G.H.Q. O.B./1866/E. This entailed a reduction of 36 Drivers and 72 animals on the previous establishment.	
	24/6/18		OFFICERS. Lieut. F.H. THOMPSON was posted to 32nd Div. T.M. Batteries on this date.	
	25/6/18.		ATTACHMENTS. No. 1 Section, 40th D.A.C. came under this units direction on this date.	
			AMMUNITION TRANSACTIONS. during the month have been:-	
			18.pr 4.5" Gas, etc. Receipts. 65088 17990 3200 Issues. 65221 19903 3237	
			REINFORCEMENTS. 66 reinforcements have joined during the month and have been distributed to units of the 32nd Divisional Artillery.	
			LOCATION. Location of this unit at end of the month, GOUY-EN-ARTOIS.	

Lieut. Col.
Commdg. 32nd. Div. Ammn. Col., R.F.A.

Confidential

War Diary

of

32nd Divisional Ammunition Column
R F A

From :- 1st July 1918
To :- 31st July 1918

Army Form C. 2118

WAR DIARY
or
INTELLIGENCE SUMMARY

JULY 1918.

(Erase heading not required.)

Instructions regarding War Diaries and Intelligence Summaries are contained in F.S. Regs., Part II. and the Staff Manual respectively. Title Pages will be prepared in manuscript.

32ND DIVISIONAL AMMUNITION COLUMN R.F.A.

Place	Date	Hour	Summary of Events and Information	Remarks and references to Appendices
In the Field.	1/7/18		HONOURS AND AWARDS. No. 21673, B.S.M. BLOWMAN, J.? of this unit was awarded the Meritorious Service Medal. Vide London Gazette, June 1918.	
-do-	1/7/18		OFFICERS. 2/Lieut. A. WELLS, R.F.A. (S.R.) taken on the strength from 32nd Division T.M. Batteries.	
-do-	4/7/18		MOVES. H.Q. and No. 2 Section of this unit moved to HUMBERCOURT (Sheet 51 c. Ref. U.8.a.) on relief by Guards Div. Amm. Col.	
-do-	7/7/18		S.A.A. Section of this unit moved to BAVINCOURT and on the 12th instant to HUMBERCOURT.	
-do-	13/7/18		HONOURS AND AWARDS. No. 78278, L/Bdr. J. GIBBONS of this unit was awarded the Military Medal by G.O.C., VI Corps for gallant conduct whilst in charge of a forward Infantry ammunition dump, bombed by E.A.	
-do-	16/7/18		No. 32573, Sergt. C.B. TAWN and No. L/13891, Driver H. DALTON of this unit were awarded gallantry cards by G.O.C., 32nd Division for meritorious conduct in connection with the shelling of one of this unit's ammunition convoys.	
-do-	17/7/18		MOVES. No. 1 Section of this unit moved to HUMBERCOURT.	
-do-	19/7/18		The unit complete entrained at DOULLENS and BOUQUEMAISON for Second Army Area, detrained at HOVEN on 20/7/18 and went into camps in II Corps Reserve Area.	
-do-	22/7/18		DUMPS. A reserve ammunition dump named LOVIE CHATEAU Dump was taken over by this unit from the 65th DAC.	
-do-	26/7/18		DETACHMENTS. 3 Officers and 90 other ranks of this unit were attached to 6th and 41st Divisional Artilleries for digging operations, etc.	
-do-	30/7/18		CASUALTIES. 2 other ranks wounded.	
			AMMUNITION TRANSACTIONS. during the month were as follows:-
			18 pr 4.5" Gas, etc.
			Received. 30,504 8100 1100 } includes dumps'
			Issued. 8,688 1756 1490 } transactions.
			REINFORCEMENTS. 97 reinforcements joined during the month and were posted to units of 32nd D.A.	
			LOCATION. At the end of the month, the unit's H.Q. was at Sheet 27, E.17.b.8.8.	

J. Wellin Lieut. Col.
Commdg. 32nd. Div. Ammn. Col., R.F.A.

Confidential

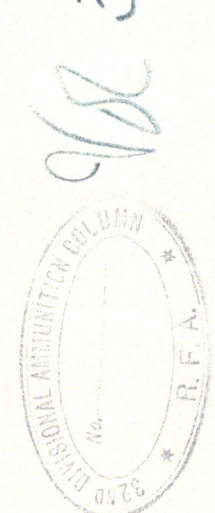

War Diary
— of —
32nd Divisional Ammunition Column R.F.A.

Period 1st to 31st August. 1918.

Sheet 2

Army Form C. 2118

WAR DIARY
or
INTELLIGENCE SUMMARY August 1918

(Erase heading not required.)

Place	Date	Hour	Summary of Events and Information	Remarks and references to Appendices
In the Field	Aug 29th		<u>Dump:</u> A Forward Grenade Dump was formed at T.8.c.0.5 (Sheet 62c)	
-do-	-do-		The A.R.P. was moved by lorries to S.4.b. Central (Sheet 62c)	
-do-	Aug 30th		<u>Casualties.</u> 2 O.R's wounded; hostile mine.	
			<u>Ammunition</u> A AX BX Gas R.	
			<u>Transactions.</u> Received. 36,698 28,962 17,612 14,128	
			Issued. 32,948 26,689 16,926 13,448	
			<u>Reinforcements.</u> 115 reinforcements joined the unit during the month and were distributed to units of 32nd Divisional Artillery.	
			<u>Location of Unit.</u> H.Q. at end of the month. VAUVILLERS. (N.E.C. Ref. Sheet 62 D)	

J. Walker, Lt. Col.
Commdg. 32nd Div. Ammn. Coln. R.F.A.

Army Form C. 2118

WAR DIARY or INTELLIGENCE SUMMARY

(Erase heading not required.)

August 1918

Place	Date	Hour	Summary of Events and Information	Remarks and references to Appendices
In the field	Aug 7th		Officer: Lieut. C.E. FOTHERBY struck off the strength: admitted hospital England 31-7-18	for
-do-	Aug 8th		Moves: The unit complete entrained at HERDEBEEK (Ref. Sheet 19. X.21.c.9.2) and detrained at SALEUX (Ref. AMIENS Sheet.2.c) and HANGEST (Ref. AMIENS Sheet.1.A) and proceeded by march route to H.Q. to CAGNY (Ref. AMIENS Sheet.2.E) one Section to AMIENS, two Sections to LONGUEAU (Ref. AMIENS Sheet.2.E).	for
-do-	Aug 9th		The unit proceeded to neighbourhood of DOMART (Ref. Sheet 62.D. X.27.d.)	for
-do-	Aug 10th		The unit proceeded to vicinity of LE QUESNEL (Ref. Sheet 66.E. D.30. Cent and K.8.c)	for
-do-	Aug 13th		S.A.A Section of this unit moved to DOMART.	for
-do-	Aug 19th		The unit complete left Canadian Corps area and moved to Australian Corps area, H.Q. + Sections being established in vicinity of P.35.A. (Sheet 62D).	for
-do-	Aug 20th		This unit took over an A.R.P. at P.35.c (Sheet 62D) from 2nd Aus. D.A.C.	for
-do-	Aug 23rd		Moves: No's 1, 2, and S.A.A. Sections moved to vicinity of HARBONNIERES (Ref. Sheet 62.D. W.18.a)	for
-do-	-do-		No's 1 and 2 Sections moved to FRAMERVILLE (Ref. Sheet 62.D. X.2.c)	for
-do-	-do-		No's 1 and 2 Sections moved to HERLEVILLE (Ref. Sheet 62.D. X.6.c.)	for
-do-	Aug 29th		H.Q. moved to VAUVILLERS (Ref. Sheet 62.D. X.8.c.)	for
-do-	-do-		S.A.A. Section moved to HERLEVILLE	for

Army Form C. 2118

WAR DIARY
or
INTELLIGENCE SUMMARY — August 1918

(Erase heading not required.)

Instructions regarding War Diaries and Intelligence Summaries are contained in F.S. Regs., Part II. and the Staff Manual respectively. Title Pages will be prepared in manuscript.

Place	Date	Hour	Summary of Events and Information	Remarks and references to Appendices
In the Field	Aug 4th		Officer. Lieut. G.E. FOTHERBY struck off the Strength: admitted hospital England 31-7-18	
-do-	Aug 5th		Moves. The unit complete entrained at HERDEBEEK (Ref. Sheet 19.X.21.c.9.2) and detrained at SALEUX (Ref. Amiens Sheet 2.c) and HANGEST (Ref. Amiens Sheet 1.A) and proceeded by march route to H.Q. to CAGNY (Ref. Amiens Sheet 2.E) one section to AMIENS, two sections to LONGUEAU (Ref. Amiens Sheet 2E)	
-do-	Aug 9th		The unit proceeded to neighbourhood of DOMART (Ref. Sheet 62.D.X.27.A.)	
-do-	Aug 10th		The unit proceeded to vicinity of LE QUESNEL (Ref. Sheet 66E. D.30.Cent. and K.8.c)	
-do-	Aug 13th		S.A.A Section of this unit moved to DOMART.	
-do-	Aug 19		The unit complete left Canadian Corps area and moved to Australian Corps area, H.Q. & Sections being established in vicinity of P.35.a. (Sheet 62D)	
-do-	Aug 20th		Dumps. This unit took over an A.R.P. at R.35.c (Sheet 62D) from 2nd Aus. D.A.C.	
-do-	Aug 28th		Moves. No's 1, 2, and S.A.A. Sections moved to vicinity of HARBONNIERES (Ref. Sheet 62D W.18.a.)	
-do-	-do-		No's 1 and 2 Sections moved to FRAMERVILLE (Ref. Sheet 62.D. X.2.c)	
-do-	-do-		No's 1 and 2 Sections moved to HERLEVILLE (Ref. Sheet 62.D X.8.c)	
-do-	Aug 29		H.Q. moved to VAUVILLERS (Ref. Sheet 62D X.8.c)	
-do-	-do-		S.A.A Section moved to HERLEVILLE	

VM 33

Confidential

War Diary
-of-
32nd Divisional Ammunition Column R.F.A.

Period:— 1st to 30th September 1918.

WAR DIARY
or
INTELLIGENCE SUMMARY

(Erase heading not required.)

SEPTEMBER 1918.

Army Form C. 2118

Place	Date	Hour	Summary of Events and Information	Remarks and references to Appendices
In The Field	1918 Sep. 5/6		**MOVE.** The Unit complete, (less S.A.A. Section) moved from VAUVILLERS to BRIOST, opposite St.Christ on the Somme Canal, on the advance of the 32nd Division.	
	8th		The Unit moved from BRIOST to MONCHY-LAGACHE? BETWEEN THE Somme Canal and ST.QUENTIN on the 32nd Division continuing to move forward. Ammunition dumps were moved forward, as the Unit advanced, in each case.	
	14th		**OFFICERS.** 2/Lieut. G.P. Walton, R.F.A. joined this Unit from Base.	
	18th		**CASUALTIES.** 1 o.r. killed by enemy aircraft bomb. 1 o.r. wounded -do-	
	24th		**ADJUTANCY.** A/Capt. J.E. Johnson relinquished the appointment of Adjutant of this Unit, and was posted to Nº 1 Section. Tempy. Lieut. F. Wisher, M.C., was appointed Adjutant of the Unit in the vacancy above created.	
	25th		**CASUALTIES.** 1 o.r. wounded by enemy shell fire.	
	29th		**MOVE.** On the advance of the 32nd Division over the Canal North West of ST. QUENTIN, this Unit moved forward to VADENCOURT, north West of ST. QUENTIN. S.A.A. Section of the Unit moved forward to the vicinity of LE VERGUIER, and moved the next day to LA BARAQUE, crossing the Canal North of ST.QUENTIN. 1 officer and 5 o.r. trained in the service of the German 77 mm. gun, were attached to 161st Brigade R.F.A. and moved forward on the advance, in case they could be used should opportunity occur. They were used to advance with the Infantry and fired a number of rounds from a captured German 77 gun.	
	30th		**CASUALTIES.** 1 O:R: wounded by enemy shell fire.	
			AMMUNITION transactions during the month were as under:- 18pr. 4.5" Gas. etc. Receipts:- 78,911 23,218 8984) Includes handing over Issues:- 78,229 22,599 8886) transactions.	

WAR DIARY
or
INTELLIGENCE-SUMMARY

(Erase heading not required.)

Army Form C. 2118

SEPTEMBER 1918. Page 2;

[Stamp: 32ND DIVISIONAL AMMUNITION COLUMN R.F.A.]

Instructions regarding War Diaries and Intelligence Summaries are contained in F. S. Regs., Part II. and the Staff Manual respectively. Title Pages will be prepared in manuscript.

Place	Date	Hour	Summary of Events and Information	Remarks and references to Appendices
			REINFORCEMENTS. 118 Reinforcements joined this Unit from Base during the month and was distributed to Units of 32nd Divisional Artillery. LOCATION of Units H.Q. at end of the month, R.10.c.9;1, sheet 62C.	for /18
			J. Walker Lieut. Col. Commdg. 32n l. Div. Ammn. Col., R.F.A.	

1875 Wt. W.593/826 1,000,000 4/15 J.B.C. & A. A.D.S.S./Forms/C. 2118.

Confidential

War Diary
– of –
32nd Divisional Ammunition Column,
– R.F.A. –

From 1st October 1918.
To   31st October 1918.

Army Form C. 2118.

WAR DIARY
or
INTELLIGENCE SUMMARY.   OCTOBER 1918.
(Erase heading not required.)

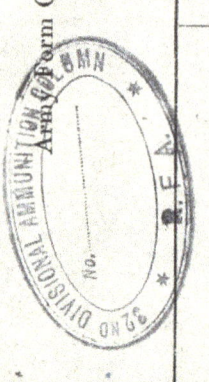

Place	Date	Hour	Summary of Events and Information	Remarks and references to Appendices
In the Field.	Oct.7th		OFFICERS. Capt. F.D. SMITH, A.V.C. struck off the strength on proceeding to Canada for 42 days leave	W.W.W.W.
	Oct.8th		Capt. R.J. BEWELL, R.F.A. joined from Base Depot.	W.W.W.
-do-	Oct.10th		INDIAN PERSONNEL. 150 O.R's Native Indian personnel joined this unit for duty from Indian Base Depot.	W.W.W.
-do-	Oct.11th		CASUALTIES. 1 O.R. of Indian Native personnel accidentally killed (S.I.) by explosion of German Hand Grenade.	W.W.W.
-do-	Oct.15th		MOVES. The unit (less S.A.A. Section) moved forward to vicinity of BRANCOURT (N.W. of BOHAIN) and was attached to the 6th Divisional Artillery.	W.W.W.
-do-	Oct.16th		CASUALTIES. 1 other rank wounded by enemy fire.	W.W.W.
-do-	Oct.16th		OFFICERS. Capt. PAUL, A.V.C. joined this unit as Veterinary Officer.	W.W.W.
-do-	Oct.19th Oct.20th		MOVES. The unit (less S.A.A. Section) moved to the vicinity of BUSIGNY (N. of BOHAIN) and was attached to the 1st Divisional Artillery until 31st October 1918.	W.W.W. W.W.W.
-do-	Oct.21st		S.A.A. Section of this unit moved to BOHAIN	W.W.
-do-	Oct.22nd		CASUALTIES. 1 other rank wounded by enemy shell fire (died on 23rd)	W.W.W.
-do-	Oct.31st		MOVES. S.A.A. Section of this unit moved to ESCAUFORT.	W.W.

AMMUNITION TRANSACTIONS during the month are as follows:-

	18 pr	4.5"	Gas, etc.
Receipts	45,906	11,684	4850
ISSUES.	55,512	14,730	5372
Salved and picked up from abandoned gun positions.	23,176	7224	1768

REINFORCEMENTS. 178 reinforcements joined from the Base and were distributed to units of 32nd Divisional Artillery.

LOCATION of unit's H.Q. at end of the month. BUSIGNY, V.17.c.2.9. (Sheet 57b)

W.W. Lucas Col. Lieut.-Col.
Commdg. 32nd. Div. Ammn. Col, R.F.A.

Confidential

Vol 35

War Diary.

of

32nd Divisional Ammunition Column
R.F.A.

Period :- 1st to 30th November 1918.

Army Form C.2118.

WAR DIARY
or
INTELLIGENCE SUMMARY.

(Erase heading not required.)

NOVEMBER 1918.

32nd DIVISIONAL AMMUNITION COLUMN R.F.A.

Place	Date	Hour	Summary of Events and Information	Remarks and references to Appendices
In the Field.	1918 Nov. 2nd		CASUALTIES. 1 o.r. (Indian personnel) wounded by enemy shell fire.	
	4th		MOVES. N° 2 Section of the Unit moved to ST. BENIN (near LE CATEAU).	
	6th		" S.A.A. Section -do- -do- BASUEL (East of LE CATEAU).	
	"		" HdQrs. -do- -do- BASUEL.	
	"		" N° 1 Section -do- -do- BASUEL.	
	"		" N° 2 Section and S.A.A. Section of the Unit moved over the SAMBRE and OISE Canal to SAMBRETON, East of CATTILLON.	
	8th		" S.A.A. Section and N° 2 Section of the Unit moved forward to vicinity of FAVRIL in the direction of AVESNES.	
	9th		" H.Q. and N° 1 Section of the Unit moved to FAVRIL and S.A.A. Section to GRAND FAYT.	
	"		" N° 2 Section of the Unit moved to MAR BAIX.	
	11th		ARMISTICE with enemy with effect from 11.00 hours this day.	
	12th		MOVES. Unit less N° 2 Section moved to outskirts of AVESNES.	
	"		" N° 2 Section moved to SEMERIES, East of AVESNES.	
	16th		" S.A.A. Section of Unit moved to SAINS DU NORD, East of AVESNES.	
	18th		INDIAN PERSONNEL. 59 o.r. of the Indian personnel attached to this Unit, were on this day dispatched to Indian R.A. Advanced Base Depôt in consequence of it being decided to take as few Indian personnel as possible on the march forward.	
	19th		MOVES. The 32nd Division commenced march to RHINE area.	
	"		" This Unit complete marched to SIVRY (on Belgian Border).	
	20th		" Unit continued march to FOURBECHIES.	
	24th		" Unit continued march to CERFONTAINE.	
			Unit remained at CERFONTAINE until the end of the month.	

Army Form C. 2118.

WAR DIARY
or
INTELLIGENCE SUMMARY.   NOVEMBER 1918. (page 2).
(Erase heading not required.)

Instructions regarding War Diaries and Intelligence Summaries are contained in F. S. Regs., Part II. and the Staff Manual respectively. Title pages will be prepared in manuscript.

[Stamp: 32ND DIVISIONAL AMMUNITION COLUMN R.F.A.]

Place	Date	Hour	Summary of Events and Information	Remarks and references to Appendices
In the Field	1918 Novr.		AMMUNITION TRANSACTIONS up to the 11th November were as follows:-	
			18-pdr. 4.5"	
			Receipts:- 7,426 1,991.	
			Issues:- 6,723 2,066.	
			REINFORCEMENTS. 24 Reinforcements joined the Unit from Base and were distributed to Units of 32nd Divisional Artillery.	

                                                                       J. Walker   Lieut. Col.
                                                              Commdg. 32nd. Div. Ammn. Col., R.F.A.

Confidential

War Diary

of

32nd Divisional Ammunition Column R.F.A.

Period:- 1st to 31st December 1918.

WAR DIARY
or
INTELLIGENCE SUMMARY.
(Erase heading not required.)

Army Form C. 2118.

32ND DIVISIONAL AMMUNITION COLUMN R.F.A.

DECEMBER 1918.

Instructions regarding War Diaries and Intelligence Summaries are contained in F.S. Regs., Part II. and the Staff Manual respectively. Title pages will be prepared in manuscript.

Place	Date	Hour	Summary of Events and Information	Remarks and references to Appendices
In the field	1918. Dec. 7th		AWARDS. Notification was received that Indian Driver JUMMA of this Unit had been awarded the Indian Distinguished Service Medal for gallant conduct.	/s/
	12th		MOVES. Unit complete commenced march to NAMUR area and on this day moved from CEM FONTAINE to MORTAGNE.	/s/
	13th		" Move continued to LESVES.	
	14th		" Move continued to destination, the Unit being accommodated in the LENTRY – FAULX – SART BERNARD area in the neighbourhood of NAMUR.	/s/
	17th		NOTICES. 2/Lieut. J.W. Large taken on the strength from 158th Brigade R.F.A.	/s/
			EDUCATION. Educational Classes were commenced in the Unit, dealing with various subjects, e.g. Agriculture and Veterinary, First-aid, French, Shorthand, etc.	/s/
	23rd		DEMOBILIZATION. The first parties of men from this Unit were dispatched for demobilization, and consisted principally of former civil policemen and miners. Up to the end of the month, 74 other ranks had been dispatched for demobilization.	/s/
	28th		SALVAGE. A Party of 4 Officers and 120 O.R. from the Unit with animals and wagons, were attached to 97th Infantry Brigade to carry out salvage work in the Divisional area.	/s/
			REINFORCEMENTS. 5 Reinforcements joined the Unit and were posted to Units of 32nd Div.Artillery.	/s/
			LOCATION of Unit H.Q. at end of month: Chateau d'Arville, near NAMUR.	/s/

J. Walker Lieut. Col.
Commdg. 32nd. Div. Ammn. Col., R.F.A.

LANCASHIRE DIVISION
(LATE 32ND DIVN)

32ND DIVL AMMN COLMN
JAN - OCT 1919

LANCASHIRE DIVISION
(LATE 32ND DIVN)

Confidential

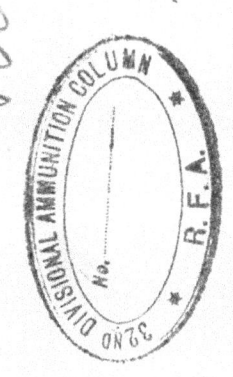

War Diary
— of —

32nd Divisional Ammunition Column R.F.A.

Period. 1st to 31st January 1919.

Army Form C. 2118.

WAR DIARY
or
INTELLIGENCE=SUMMARY.
(Erase heading not required.)

JANUARY 1919.

Instructions regarding War Diaries and Intelligence Summaries are contained in F. S. Regs., Part II. and the Staff Manual respectively. Title pages will be prepared in manuscript.

Place	Date	Hour	Summary of Events and Information	Remarks and references to Appendices
In the Field.	1919 Jan. 10		DEMOBILIZATION. 8 o.r. were dispatched from the Unit for dispersal.	
	12		" " 7 o.r. were dispatched from the Unit for dispersal.	
	17		" " 1 officer and 17 o.r. were dispatched from the Unit for dispersal.	
	19		" " 13 o.r. were dispatched from the Unit for dispersal.	
	21		" " 10 o.r. were dispatched from the Unit for dispersal.	
	27		AWARDS. Notification was received of the Award of the Meritorious Service Medal to RGA/79427 Sergt. J. Coltman of the Unit.	
	28		DEMOBILIZATION. The Commanding Officer of the Unit, Lieut-Col. J. Walker, D.S.O. this day proceeded to England for demobilization.	
	29		COMMAND. Command of the Unit was taken over by Capt. W.W.M. Tweedie, R.F.A.	
			Nil Reinforcements joined the Unit during the month.	
			LOCATION of Unit's H.Q. at end of the month - Chateau d'Arville, near NAMUR.	

Capt & Adjutant,
For Officer Commanding,
32nd Div. Ammtn. Col. R.F.A.

Confidential

War Diary

of

32nd Divisional Ammunition Column R.F.A.

Period 1st to 28th February 1919.

Army Form C. 2118.

WAR DIARY
or
INTELLIGENCE SUMMARY.
(Erase heading not required.)

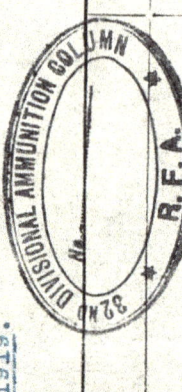

Instructions regarding War Diaries and Intelligence Summaries are contained in F. S. Regs., Part II. and the Staff Manual respectively. Title pages will be prepared in manuscript.

Place	Date	Hour	Summary of Events and Information	Remarks and references to Appendices
Bonn Germany	1919 Feb. 2nd to 5th		MOVES. During these dates, the Unit moved by rail from the NAMUR area to BONN, Germany, where the Unit was accommodated in the Kaiser Wilhelm Kaserne, Bonn.	W.S.M
	10th		REWARDS. Notification received that No. 23312 Driver T. Booth had been awarded the Military Medal for bravery in the Field (whilst serving with another Unit). Supp. to London Gazette dated 28/1/19.	W.S.M
	15th		DISBANDMENT of 32nd Division Medium Trench Mortar Batteries took place on this day and the personnel which had formed these batteries, was posted to this Unit.	W.S.M
	15th		OFFICERS. Lieut. R.H. Thompson R.F.A. (TF) posted to this Unit from 32nd T.M. Batteries.	W.S.M
	18th		INSPECTION. An inspection of the Unit was made on this date by the M.G., Royal Artillery, Second Army.	W.S.M
	22nd		REWARDS. No. 15806 Sergt. A.S. Hornby of this Unit awarded the Military Medal. (Peace Honours Dispatch).	W.S.M
			DEMOBILIZATION. 7 o.r. were dispatched for demobilization during the month.	W.S.M
			REINFORCEMENTS. Nil Reinforcements joined the Unit during the month.	W.S.M

W.S...
Major
Lieut. Col.
Commdg. 32nd. Div. Ammn. Col., R.F.A.

Confidential

War Diary
of
Lancashire (32nd) Divisional Ammunition Column R.F.A.

Period 1st to 31st March 1919.

Army Form C. 2118.

WAR DIARY
or
INTELLIGENCE SUMMARY. MARCH 1919.
(Erase heading not required.)

Instructions regarding War Diaries and Intelligence Summaries are contained in F. S. Regs., Part II. and the Staff Manual respectively. Title pages will be prepared in manuscript.

Place	Date	Hour	Summary of Events and Information	Remarks and references to Appendices
Form Germany	1919 March 1st		OFFICERS. Lieut. A. Wells struck off the strength on leave in England being extended pending demobilization.	WM
	15th		DESIGNATION. The designation of this Unit is changed to Lancashire Divisional Ammunition Column, on 32nd Division being re-named Lancashire Division.	WM
	19th		OFFICERS. The command of S.A.A. Section of this Unit was taken over by Lieut. J. J. Hooper R.G.A. with the acting rank of Capt. R.F.A.	WM
			No other events in connection with the Unit occurred during the remainder of the month which were worthy of record.	WM
			REINFORCEMENTS. 224 Reinforcements joined this Unit during the month, and were distributed to Units of Lancashire Divisional Artillery.	WM
			DEMOBILIZATION. 1 Officer and 35 o.r. were dispatched from this Unit during the month for demobilization.	WM

W.M. Major.
Comm'dg. Lanc's. Div. Ammn. Col. R.F.A.

WAR DIARY or INTELLIGENCE SUMMARY.

Army Form C. 2118.

(Erase heading not required.)

Place	Date 1919.	Hour	Summary of Events and Information	Remarks and references to Appendices
KOLN. Germany.	April 14th.		ADJUTANCY. Lieut. F.W. Giles appointed Adjutant of the Unit.	
	15th.		COMMAND. Command of the Unit was taken over by Major H.W. Pollock M.C. R.F.A. (T)	
	26th.		INSPECTION. This Unit, with the Batteries of the Lancs. Divisional Artillery was inspected by the C.R.A. at WAHRELAR, and received a favourable report.	
			No other events in connection with the Unit occurred during the remainder of the month which were worthy of record.	
			REINFORCEMENTS. 348 reinforcements joined this Unit during the month.	
			DEMOBILIZATION. 5 Officers and 295 o.r.'s were dispatched from this Unit during the month for demobilization.	

Major,
Commdg. Lancs. Div. Ammn. Col. R. F. A.

Army Form C. 2118.

WAR DIARY
or
INTELLIGENCE SUMMARY.
(Erase heading not required.)

Instructions regarding War Diaries and Intelligence Summaries are contained in F.S. Regs., Part II. and the Staff Manual respectively. Title pages will be prepared in manuscript.

Place	Date 1919. May.	Hour	Summary of Events and Information	Remarks and references to Appendices
BONN, Germany.	4th		COMMAND. Major W.W.M. TWEEDIE (R.F.A. Temp) resumed Command of this unit.	
	11th		INSPECTION. This unit was inspected by G.O.C. Division at Cavalry Barracks.	
	13th		INSPECTION. This unit with the batteries of the Lancashire Div.Arty.was inspected by C in C. Army of the Rhine at Hangelar Aerodrome and received a favourable report.	
			OFFICERS.	
	7th		Lieut. Randall, E.L. (R.F.A. S.R) posted to this unit from R.A. Reinforcement Camp	
	8th		Capt. Knowles, H.S. (R.F.A.Temp) " " " " " "	
	19th		Lieut. Murray, J.I. (R.F.A. S.R.) " " " " " "	
	22nd		Lieut. Jones, M.R.M. (R.F.A. S.R.) " " " " 161 Brigade, R.F.A.	
	22nd		2/Lieut. Willoughby FJ. (R.F.A. S.R.) " " " " 168 " "	
	23rd		2/Lieut. Southern, W.H. (R.F.A. S.R.) " " " " 168 " "	
	24th		Capt. Ashendan, H.G. (R.F.A. T.F.) " " " " R.A. Reinforcement Camp.	
			(M.C.)	
	26th		Lieut. Stuart, C. (R.F.A Temp) " " " " 161 Brigade, R.F.A.	
			No other events in connection with the unit occurred during the remainder of month which were worthy of record.	
			REINFORCEMENTS.	
			81 Reinforcements joined this unit during the month.	
			DEMOBILIZATION.	
			3 Officers and 6 other ranks were despatched from this unit during the month for demobilization.	

Army Form C. 2118.

WAR DIARY
or
INTELLIGENCE SUMMARY.
(Erase heading not required.)

Instructions regarding War Diaries and Intelligence Summaries are contained in F. S. Regs., Part II. and the Staff Manual respectively. Title pages will be prepared in manuscript.

Place	Date	Hour	Summary of Events and Information	Remarks and references to Appendices
BONN.	18th June 1919.		MOVE. S.A.A. Section of this unit moved to SIEGBURG.	
	19th.		No. 1 Section of this unit moved to RAMERSDORF.	
	23rd.		No. 2 Section of this unit moved to PLATO BRICKWORKS, G.Z.3.-9.7.	
	24th.		ENEMY notified officialy intentions to sign peace.	
	28th.		MOVE. Nos. 1 and 2 Sections, of this unit, returned to Cavalry Barracks, BONN.	
			PEACE. signed 15.50 hours.	
			OFFICERS.	
	6th.		2/Lieut. W.A. PYKE R.F.A. S.R. joined.	
	12th.		Lieut. L.J. COOKE R.F.A. S.R. joined.	
	17th.		Capt. H.C. ASHENDAN M.C. to England to report in writing to W.O.	
	18th.		A/Mjr. H.E. POLLOCK. M.C. " " " " " " " "	
			Capt. R.J. BEWELL " " " " " " " "	
			A/Capt. J.J. HOOPER " " " " " " " "	
	24th.		Capt. G. COSNOLD M.C. " " " " " " " "	
	27th.		Lieut. G.F. ADAMS " " " " " " " "	

W.J. Sundin, Major
Officer Commanding,
Lancs. Div. Ammt. Col. R.F.A.

Army Form C. 2118.

WAR DIARY
or
INTELLIGENCE SUMMARY.
(Erase heading not required.)

Instructions regarding War Diaries and Intelligence Summaries are contained in F. S. Regs., Part II. and the Staff Manual respectively. Title pages will be prepared in manuscript.

Place	Date	Hour	Summary of Events and Information	Remarks and references to Appendices
BONN.	July. 1919			
Germany.	21st.		OFFICERS :- A/Capt. and Adj. B.W. GILES, R.F.A. Reg. proceeded to U.K. to report in writing to War Office, and is struck off the strength.	
	20th.		ANIMALS :- 9 Ride Horses and 42 mules were dispatched to XtI. Corps A.C.C. for sale locally.	
			No other events in connection with the unit occurred during the month which were worthy of record.	

W.H.Lumdin. Major,
Commdg. Lancs. Div. Ammn. Col. R.F.A.

31/7/19.

Army Form C. 2118

WAR DIARY
or
INTELLIGENCE SUMMARY

(Erase heading not required.)

Lancashire Divisional Ammn. Col. R.F.A.

Instructions regarding War Diaries and Intelligence Summaries are contained in F.S. Regs., Part II. and the Staff Manual respectively. Title Pages will be prepared in manuscript.

Place	Date	Hour	Summary of Events and Information	Remarks and references to Appendices
BONN Germany.	August 1919.			
	10th.	15.30	VISIT. Major-General Sir W.H. Birkbeck, K.C.B., C.M.G., Director of Remounts from War Office and D.D.F., Rhine Army, accompanied by the Horse Adviser, Xth. Corps visited the stables of the unit. The Director of Remounts expressed great appreciation of the condition and appearance of the Mules of the D.A.C.	
	12th.		INSPECTION. The C.R.A., Lancashire Division inspected the unit, a congratulary report on the very high state of efficiency of the unit being received.	
	14th.		Inspection by Divisional Commander.	
			OFFICERS. Adjutancy :- Lieut. E.L. Randall, R.F.A., S.R. to be adjutant and to be acting Captain whilst so employed, 22/7/19.	
			Capt. W.F. Cooper M.C. joined from 160th. Bde. R.F.A. 6/8/19. Lieut. M.R.M. Jones struck off the strength 3/8/19 on reporting to the War Office in writing. Lieut. C. Stuart posted to "G" Battery, A.A. on 11/7/19.	
			DEMOBILIZATION 19 Other Ranks proceeded for demobilization during the month.	
			ANIMALS. 13 Riders sent to Xth. Corps A.C.C. for sale 7th. August -19. 1 Rider " " " " " 27th. " " 59 mules)	

Major,
Commdg. Lancs. Div. Ammn. Col. R.F.A.

Army Form C. 2118.

WAR DIARY
or
INTELLIGENCE SUMMARY.
(Erase heading not required.)

Instructions regarding War Diaries and Intelligence Summaries are contained in F. S. Regs., Part II. and the Staff Manual respectively. Title pages will be prepared in manuscript.

Place	Date	Hour	Summary of Events and Information	Remarks and references to Appendices
	October, 1919.			
	28th		**MOVE.**	
			No. 2 Section, complete with Officers, men, horses and equipment proceeded to join Southern Divisional Ammunition Column, R.F.A.	
			DEMOBILIZATION.	
			58 O.Rs. proceeded for demobilization during the month.	
			No other events in connection with the Unit occurred during the month which were worthy of record.	

W.M. Sundi. Major, R.F.A.
Commanding Lancashire Divisional Ammunition Column, R.F.A.

www.ingramcontent.com/pod-product-compliance
Lightning Source LLC
Chambersburg PA
CBHW081433160426
43193CB00013B/2270